To Trisha,
Are you still a
With...

LOST NORFOLK

LOST NORFOLK

AMY WATERS YARSINSKE

Published by The History Press
Charleston, SC 29403
www.historypress.net

Unless otherwise attributed, photos are in the collection of the author.

First published 2009

Manufactured in the United States

ISBN 978.1.59629.850.7

Library of Congress Cataloging-in-Publication Data

Yarsinske, Amy Waters, 1963-
Lost Norfolk / Amy Waters Yarsinske.
p. cm.
Includes bibliographical references.
ISBN 978-1-59629-850-7
1. Norfolk (Va.)--History--Pictorial works. 2. Historic buildings--Virginia--Norfolk--Pictorial works. 3. Streets--Virginia--Norfolk--History--Pictorial works. 4. Central business districts--Virginia--Norfolk--History--Pictorial works. 5. City and town life--Virginia--Norfolk--History--Pictorial works. 6. Norfolk (Va.)--Buildings, structures, etc.--Pictorial works. I. Title.
F234.N8Y355 2009
975.5'521--dc22
2009038603

CONTENTS

PREFACE

With over three centuries of rich history, Norfolk has a story to tell but little left to show for it. While all is not lost, all is not there. This is the story of what was, of people who experienced the city in a different time than our own. Pictures speak a thousand words; they speak to buildings, events of local to international importance and to the people who made Norfolk a vibrant, dynamic place to live and work in days gone by. But pictures also do something else: they remind us of what could have been. Throughout this book there will be photographs that make you stop and think, "That's still there." But look again. Something else has changed, perhaps a streetscape, the context of the building or the people in the street. The way we see it "now" may not be how we remember it "when." This harks back to an old way of seeing the past as part of the present.

The razing of many of the city's most historically and architecturally significant buildings during post–World War II redevelopment—a practice that continues even today—has detached people from the past, from an appreciation for what was and connectivity with a sustainable, historically significant built environment, as well as from a sense of place. There was a time when one could walk down any Norfolk street and find buildings that fit together harmoniously, but more than that, the buildings were alive in their surroundings as much as the people moving in and out of and around them. The streets of Norfolk stopped being joyfully alive after World War II. Gone is the appreciation for history, tradition and southern culture that tourists and residents alike find so appealing in destinations like Charleston,

South Carolina, or Annapolis's charming streets, tucked intimately close to the water. Architect and author Jonathan Hale observed that what attracts him most about old buildings is not their quaintness or the knowledge of what happened in them—not age or history. "I am attracted to what I call their smile," he wrote in 1994, "their slightly mysterious *presence*." This way of seeing buildings in the context of their environment started fading from American design starting in the Victorian era, and with it went the magic that, Hale later concluded, was "that old feeling of being in a real place."

Context is only part of it. There is certainly something intrinsically wrong with siting new buildings in an old city when they wipe their aged neighbors off the block. In trying to make the city come alive again, there is a tendency to make buildings that are about other places, Hale cautioned. But was anyone listening? Many buildings can be put down in metropolitan areas, but if they lack any component—style, color, scale, historical accuracy to the place and craftsmanship—Hale wrote, they lack rhythm with the environment, including people. They do not add to the sense of place. Norfolk fell into this trap in the 1950s and 1960s, when it traded a historic downtown in favor of an entirely new one. In the process, Norfolk lost old traditions and sacrificed the city's original footprint. Today, we replicate old styles as symbols to invoke the "lost magic" of the past. We cannot go back and make it right, but we can resist the impulse to destroy what is left and remember what our history, interpreted through our buildings, streetscapes and riverbanks, signifies in the life—and sense of place—of this old port city.

INTRODUCTION

Norfolk's earliest downtown was at the Elizabeth River waterfront, facing the harbor. Main Street ran parallel to the river along a finger-shaped piece of land bounded by the Elizabeth on the south and west and Town Back Creek to the north. The earliest industrial and commercial buildings occupied this peninsula and were grouped along the east–west axis of Main Street. Church Street intersected Main Street at its eastern end and formed the earliest north–south axis connecting Norfolk's downtown to the outlying areas. With the filling in of Town Back Creek in the 1880s, Granby Street became a prominent north–south axis as well, intersecting Main near its western end. After 1900, residential buildings along Granby were replaced by commercial structures as Granby developed into the primary shopping area of Norfolk, eclipsing Main Street as the heart of downtown. Today, Granby and Monticello are the primary north–south avenues, while Atlantic and Bank Streets are less traveled north–south routes. Cross streets (beginning at Main and continuing northward) are Plume, City Hall, Brooke, Tazewell, College Place and Freemason.

Downtown is the site of the original town and city of Norfolk. A brief overview of its early growth and development provides a historical context for some of the features and patterns that remain today. Norfolk's favorable location, adjacent to rivers and deep creeks that provided access to the ocean, was one of the primary determinants of its early development. Seventeenth-century Norfolk was a rural area of tobacco plantations whose crops were shipped to European markets. The system of inlets that existed throughout the area encouraged trading and shipping from individual plantation sites. This unorganized and decentralized system of trading was regarded with disfavor by the British government, since it made the imposition of trade regulations difficult. The king and colonial governor felt that the development of towns was necessary to regulate trade and ensure the success of its colonies; thus, in 1680, the Virginia General Assembly passed the "Act of Cohabitation and Encouragement of Trade and Manufacturing." The act required the county to establish and develop a town site. The Lower Norfolk County Court instructed its surveyor, John Ferebee, to locate and lay out a fifty-acre town site. Ferebee picked a location at the point of land where the Eastern Branch and main stem of the Elizabeth River came together, thus ensuring good water access to surrounding areas. Fifty-one lots were laid out on this property purchased from Nicholas Wise. Main Street was built on the high ground, and the town was divided into half-acre lots, which were then granted to persons agreeing to build either a dwelling or a warehouse and to pay £100 of tobacco.

The original town was almost completely surrounded by water, with penetrations along the north side by Town Back Creek and Newton's Creek. Access by land was limited to a single road, which later became Church Street. In today's context, the original town covered what is now the southern portion of downtown Norfolk, bounded generally by the river on the south and west, City Hall Avenue on the north and Lovitt Avenue (in the vicinity of today's Harbor Park) on the east. After the original lots were developed, more land was needed to satisfy demand, and Colonel Samuel Boush, Norfolk's first mayor, began subdividing and selling individual lots from his land outside the town limits as early as 1728. This tract included the area once crisscrossed by Granby, Boush, Cumberland, Market, Freemason and Bute Streets. At least one street had been mapped by 1749. Further arrangement of lots and streets was incomplete for another thirteen years. Streets named in Boush's plan, dated June 29, 1762, formed a block pattern. The continuing growth of Norfolk and its surrounding area prompted the citizens to seek enlargement of the town.

At a meeting of the House of Burgesses on August 13, 1736, several town and county residents presented a petition requesting expansion of Norfolk proper, and thus followed the town's incorporation. On September 15, 1736, a charter was adopted incorporating the borough of Norfolk, with a mayor, recorder, alderman and common council. The charter also extended Norfolk's boundaries to Town Bridge (the corner of Boush and Charlotte Streets), thereby incorporating portions of the properties owned by Samuel Boush. The boundaries were again extended in 1750, with the new boundary following the south side of Charlotte Street from Church Street to a stone on the north side of Bute Street (near 276 West Bute Street) and running parallel to Boush Street until it intersected with Brooke Avenue. Further expansion occurred in 1761, when the House passed the "Act for Enlarging and Ascertaining the Limits of the Borough of Norfolk." This extended the northern boundary to the winding body of water known as Smith's Creek (commonly called The Hague), thereby incorporating Samuel Smith's glebe land, now the West Freemason Street district, into the borough. This is the general area covered by the George Nicholson map of 1802, reputed to be the earliest complete map of Norfolk still in existence.

Throughout its early history, Norfolk went through periods of prosperity and disaster. There was extensive destruction during the Revolutionary War. The only pre–Revolutionary War building remaining in the city is Saint Paul's Episcopal Church, built in 1739. During the half century that followed the war, Norfolk changed remarkably. The commercial section was confined largely to the central and eastern sections of Main and lower Church Streets, while much of what was built toward West Main, in areas north of Town Back and Boush Creeks, today the location of City Hall Avenue, included houses and small businesses. Postwar rebuilding occurred slowly, and development was further disrupted by a dozen major fires in the first half of the nineteenth century. New land was added beyond the town's 1807 boundary, north of the present-day corner of Church Street and Princess Anne Road. Provisions were made to pave streets for the first time, also in 1807. A few streetlamps, fired by whale oil, were added in 1811, and shortly thereafter an ordinance was passed assigning a city watch to the streets, but only during the day. Gas lamps appeared on Freemason Street about 1850, and electric lighting was not introduced for another three decades.

When Norfolk became a city in 1845, its land area had grown exponentially to about 1.3 square miles, and the population exceeded ten thousand persons. The entire city at that time was only slightly larger than the present-day downtown area. Though Norfolk is rich in history from the seventeenth and early eighteenth centuries, this is not reflected architecturally. Antebellum buildings are rare in downtown Norfolk. By 1852, a triangular lot formed by the intersection of Granby, Bute and Charlotte Streets had been set aside as public green space. Plans were made to fill in Town Back Creek further and to establish a public square between Bank and Granby Streets, west of the green space at City Hall Avenue.

In 1818, a stone bridge was built across Town Back Creek from the foot of Granby Street to Concord Street, south of Back Street, thus connecting Granby Street to Main Street. This reinforced and facilitated the pattern of growth northward. Stately homes lined Granby Street until the late nineteenth to early twentieth centuries, when commercial development pushed farther down Granby Street, past City Hall Avenue and beyond Church Street. Town Back Creek, a filthy and odorous body of water to all who lived and worked near its banks, was partly filled in between 1833 and 1839 east of the Bank Street Bridge and the area now bounded by City Hall Avenue and Bank Street. Williams and Cove Streets were fenced in, planted with shade trees and designated a public square. By the mid-nineteenth century, many of downtown's landmarks had been constructed: Norfolk Academy, 1840; the city hall and courthouse (now the General Douglas A. MacArthur Memorial), 1850; Freemason Street Baptist Church, 1850; the Basilica of Saint Mary's of the Immaculate Conception, 1858; and the customhouse, designed by Ammi B. Young and also finished in 1858.

During the Civil War and Reconstruction periods, Norfolk's main commercial area, a mixture of shops and warehouses, was located along Main Street, mostly along the street's east end. The late nineteenth century was heralded as a period of opportunity and expansion. It was a time of technological and social change precipitated by the Industrial Revolution that followed closely on the heels of the Civil War. Though the post–Civil War period was a time of remarkable empire building—of the captains of industry, from financiers, railroad barons, real estate magnates, steel and oil men who were most closely identified with this era and the decades to follow—the South, slowed by the war and Reconstruction period, was less enthusiastic about this progress. Norfolk, like many southern cities, had experienced economic hardships during and immediately following the Civil War. By the 1880s, the city was just beginning to come back financially and socially. Family fortunes were rebuilt, and the city's overall economic depression lifted. Influential mid- to late nineteenth-century Norfolk families returned to seats of power and influence. Those once considered opportunists from the North, even so-called carpetbaggers, found a welcome place in the business and social life of the city. Together, they invested in Norfolk, executing improvements that would make the city competitive with commensurate industrial and port communities in the North. Town Back Creek was filled in further during the 1880s in an effort to provide developmental opportunities and to improve the drainage system. A new boulevard (now City Hall Avenue) was built from the 1850 city hall and courthouse to Granby Street; the old stone bridge at Granby Street was removed and the area was filled in to improve access to the north. While most commercial firms had previously been located along Main Street, new shops began to dot City Hall Avenue and Granby Street. In the process of commercial expansion, a number of the oldest residences in the city were demolished, soon replaced by new stores, banks and office buildings.

A significant increase in Norfolk's land area and population began taking place in the 1880s. The major factor in this growth was the installation of a street railway system. In 1866, a franchise was granted to the Norfolk City Railroad Company to lay railway tracks along city streets. The first tracks were installed on Main Street in 1869. In the following years, track lines were extended along Church and Granby Streets and through residential neighborhoods such as the West Freemason area. For the first time, workers did not have to live near their places of employment, since the trolley provided a cheap, relatively fast means of transportation. Horses pulled the first trolley cars through Norfolk's streets.

Two important technological developments contributed to changes in architectural styles that appear in Norfolk after 1880. The first innovation was the introduction of steel framing, allowing the erection of taller buildings without using massive supporting walls. Concurrently, terra cotta became popular as a decorative element. Terra cotta ornamentation, made of fine clay molded and fired into elaborate shapes, was easily mass produced. Since the terra cotta elements could be applied in pieces, it was much easier and less expensive to use than stone.

High-rise buildings, usually five to twelve stories high, were first built in the late 1890s in Norfolk. These steel-framed structures were rectangular in shape with flat roofs. Elaborate terra cotta or stone decoration was often used to highlight entrances, the first two stories and the top floors. The Citizens' Bank Building, constructed in 1899, was Norfolk's first tall, steel-framed building. Later high-rise structures notable for their terra cotta decoration include the Helena Building, the Lynnhaven Hotel, the F.S. Royster Building and the McKevitt Building. Beaux-Arts classicism, popularized by Chicago's World Columbian Exposition of 1893, ushered in an era of academic revivals. It was a strictly symmetrical style characterized by the use of clusters of columns, sculptured figures and long flights of stairs. Terra cotta again was used in elaborate decorative schemes. The former city hall (now the Seaboard Building) is a good example of Beaux-Arts classicism, which employs stone as a decorative medium. The Wells Theatre and Monticello Arcade, also of this style, exhibit elaborate terra cotta detail.

Norfolk's growth proceeded along a steady and normal path through the early 1880s, but then everything changed. The dramatic growth that followed can be directly attributed to three causes, namely western rail expansion, port and naval activity and the Jamestown Exposition of 1907. Of these determining factors, rail expansion and naval activity had the most profound, long-term impact. Although a rail line existed from 1858 connecting Norfolk to Tennessee, various factors, including the American Civil War and the Depression of 1893, combined to thwart true prosperity until about 1896, when coal field production stabilized and railroad markets expanded to include large cities as far away as Columbus, Ohio. Another railway expansion in 1901 opening up the line to Cincinnati, Ohio, meant a huge increase in business among Norfolk's port and rail lines, including new markets in the industrialized Midwest and West. The United States Navy's presence in Norfolk was palpable from the departure and return of the Great White Fleet between December 17, 1907, and February 22, 1909, and most especially after the establishment of the Norfolk Naval Station from World War I forward. The navy's effect on the city and port are best reflected in Norfolk's population and port statistics, which show this correlation clearly: Norfolk's population in 1910 was 67,452, and by 1920, it had increased to 115,777. Exports from the port in 1914 were $9.5 million and imports were $3.15 million. By 1915, exports had jumped to $19 million. In the same year, exports increased dramatically to $36 million. This was equal to the exports of San Francisco and surpassed the exports of Boston, Philadelphia and Baltimore. This growth is largely attributable to the effect of the naval base and western rail expansion during these years that had infused Norfolk with unprecedented prosperity, which was, in turn, reflected in the high style of its buildings.

Of a lesser effect, the period prior to the outbreak of World War I in Norfolk was highlighted by the Jamestown Exposition of 1907. In early 1900, a group of local businessmen convinced the Virginia General Assembly that the celebration of the 300th anniversary of the Jamestown settlement should be held in Hampton Roads. The next three years were spent raising money through the sale of stock in this private venture. Approximately 340 acres of land at Sewell's Point were later purchased, and construction began on the exposition's exhibit halls, statehouses and entertainment attractions. In effect, a miniature city was built as roads and piers were constructed, water and telephone lines installed and streets paved to go along with all of the structures erected at the site. Besides drawing thousands of people to Norfolk for the first time, the Jamestown Exposition had several lasting effects on the city. At least three new downtown hotels—the Lynnhaven, the Fairfax and the Lorraine—were built to house expected tourists.

Beyond World War I, downtown Norfolk experienced further growth that brought to the city new banks, including the Southern Bank of Norfolk, and new theatres, such as the Loew's State Theatre, one of the finest vaudeville and movie houses in the South. Granby and adjacent streets, even today, retain a number of early twentieth-century commercial structures and a few earlier buildings that survived the commercial building boom that came with the onset of urban renewal following World War II. The concentration of structures built from 1899 to 1916 include early high-rise office buildings, banks, hotels, storefronts and churches that represent the work of several of the East Coast's most prominent architects.

Norfolk continued to grow outside the downtown area. The post–World War I era included the 1923 annexation of significant portions of Norfolk's west side and bay front, pushing the city's northern boundary to the Chesapeake Bay, its eastern boundary to Poplar Hall on Broad Creek and its western boundary to Hampton Boulevard, formerly Atlantic Boulevard, and north to meet the boundary of the Norfolk Naval Station that had sprung up on land that was formerly the site of the Jamestown Exposition. Neighborhoods included in the 1923 annexation included Ballentine Place, Campostella Heights, Chesterfield Heights, Cottage Heights, Cumberland Park, Edgewater, Fairmount Park, Glenwood, Lafayette Annex, Lafayette Residence Park, Larchmont, Lenox, Lochhaven, Newton Park, Ocean View, Pine Beach, Riverfront, Westmont, Willoughby Beach and Winona. But the city was not done growing. Norfolk was the center of the ninth fastest growing metropolitan area in the United States by 1950, and with annexation of Tanner's Creek District from Norfolk County in 1955, and part of the Kempsville District of Princess Anne County in 1959, the city expanded to 61.84 square miles.

866. Market Square, Norfolk, Va.

This view of East Main Street, looking west, was taken about 1895 from Roanoke Avenue. Burk and Company (right) was a popular men's store for years. The Norfolk National Bank adjoined Burk's, and next to it was C.H. Diggs, an ice cream and candy store. The Norfolk Bank of Commerce, next to Diggs, eventually grew into Virginia National Bank, having absorbed the Norfolk National and other banks.

Opposite, top: This Kilburn Brothers stereoview of Market Square dates to 1870. When Norfolk was first surveyed in 1680, one of its primary streets was designated "the street that leadeth down to the waterside." After the market building was constructed here in the early 1700s, it became known as Market Square but also "The Parade," a drill ground. At the turn of the twentieth century, it was renamed Commercial Place. This area was half the length seen here until it was filled in with ship ballast and other materials. The market building in this picture was built on reclaimed land closer to the water and ferries.

Opposite, bottom: This tintype, circa 1860, was discovered in a vacant house being torn down at 825 Baldwin Avenue in Ghent in late 1967. The address of the residence is today the site of an addition to First Lutheran Church at 1301 Colley Avenue. Boxes of photographs remained in the house; this was rescued before the wrecking ball got the rest.

Violet Hazelton.
B.S. Campbell
21 & 23 BANK ST.
NORFOLK, VA.

Norfolk Academy, chartered in 1728, has occupied several locations in the city, among them the site shown here, circa 1892, on Bank Street. In 1806, the school's trustees purchased former Saint Paul's Episcopal Church glebe land from the Overseers of the Poor. The area, bounded by Catherine (later Bank), Charlotte and Cumberland Streets and the former Grigsby Place, sat empty until 1840, when the cornerstone of this Greek Revival Doric temple was built to accommodate Norfolk Academy's boys' school. Thomas Ustick Walter of Philadelphia, architect of the U.S. Capitol, designed it. Norfolk Academy vacated this building in 1915.

Opposite: Violet Hazelton, a trapeze artist, visited the photography studio of B.S. Campbell at 21–23 Bank Street circa 1890 to have this fine albumen portrait taken with the appropriate prop of her trade—a rope. Violet may have performed under the big top set up behind the Watt, Rettew & Clay Building, then located at the northeast corner of Main and Granby Streets, long before buildings were built at the 100 block of Granby Street. Photographer Benjamin S. Campbell, an Englishman who immigrated to the United States in 1865, produced finely detailed cabinet cards embellished with gold leaf.

William Montague Sigler was a fullback on the Norfolk Academy football team when this picture was taken on the school's front steps in 1907. This South Dakota native came to Hampton Roads when his father transferred here as a veterinary surgeon. Sigler left the area after World War I and settled in Milwaukee, Wisconsin, where he went into the automobile sales business. He died there on August 26, 1975.

The Citizens' Bank Building at 109–117 East Main Street was built from 1897 to 1899 and is the oldest tall building downtown. It is an eight-story, golden brown brick structure, trimmed with terra cotta and Worcester stone. The building was designed by renowned architect Charles E. Cassell of Baltimore, a founder of the Baltimore chapter of the American Institute of Architects (AIA). Frank R. May of Norfolk was contractor and builder. The building and site cost $200,000. Local newspapers reported that the building was occupied by January 19, 1899, the anniversary of Robert E. Lee's birth. This photograph was taken in 1900.

Patrons of the Monticello Hotel were treated to its exquisitely appointed bar, photographed by Harry C. Mann in 1908.

Opposite, top: The colonial-era home of H. Caldwell Hardy, president of the Norfolk National Bank, was built on the corner of Granby and Washington Streets, on the east side of the street with waterfront just a couple of streets between it and the bustling city waterfront. The picture shown here was taken circa 1890 by J.H. Faber. The house was razed to make way for the new Smith & Welton Department Store.

Opposite, bottom: The Monticello Hotel was built facing City Hall Avenue between Granby Street and Monticello Avenue; it opened on September 27, 1898, the same year this picture was taken. North of the hotel are stately homes and tree-lined streets that would soon succumb to large office buildings and storefronts.

WHEN AMERICA SPOKE TO THE WORLD

The Jamestown Exposition of 1907 was, in so many ways, a powerful reification of American imperialism, and President Theodore Roosevelt embodied its spirit of intent in his personal character and presidential policies abroad. With Hampton Roads—and specifically Norfolk—the centerpiece of the exposition, event organizers affirmed the United States' powerful presence on the world stage, and they did it parading America's history and national character.

To Norfolk, the Jamestown Exposition that opened on 340 acres at Sewell's Point promised large numbers of visitors to the city. The exposition grounds were accessible by streetcar from downtown; thus, in anticipation of tourists, hotel building began in earnest by 1905, although the Pine Beach Hotel and Pavilion was built as early as 1902 at a northwest angle to present-day Virginia Avenue and Gilbert Street on Norfolk Naval Station. More than thirty hotels are listed in the 1907 city directory. Three of these hotels—the Fairfax, Lorraine and Lynnhaven—remain standing today.

The Jamestown Exposition stretched from Maryland Avenue on the west to Boush Creek, which was later filled in by the United States Navy, about half a mile east of present-day Bellinger Boulevard and from Willoughby Boulevard (now Dillingham), which was then the waterfront, to Ninety-ninth (also Algonquin) Street, presently Taussig Boulevard. Due to unforeseen delays, many of the Jamestown Exposition's state buildings, main exhibition halls and amusements were unfinished when it opened on April 26, 1907. The state buildings showcased twenty-one states and two cities—Richmond, Virginia, and Baltimore, Maryland—and territories including Alaska, Panama, Puerto Rico, Cuba and the Dominican Republic. State buildings were located on the waterfront and east and west of exhibit palaces. Amusements, on the War Path, were situated on both sides of present-day Gilbert Street between Bacon Street and Commonwealth Avenue (now Farragut Avenue). The War Path resembled a carnival midway. Several of the exposition's exhibit palaces, statehouses and amusements are pictured herein, testament to an era when America spoke to the world in a compelling assemblage of American history, vibrato and naval power as the fleet went around the world on December 17, 1907.

Construction of roads, sidewalks, fences and landscaping was incomplete when this picture was taken by Jamestown Exposition Company photographer Harry C. Mann in 1907. Buildings in this picture include (left to right): Connecticut, on Willoughby Boulevard; Vermont, on Matoaka Place; U.S. Lifesaving Service, on the edge of Boush Creek; Illinois, on Bennett Circle; and Massachusetts, between Willoughby Boulevard and Bennett Circle.

The Palace of Manufactures and Liberal Arts, pictured just after dark, was photographed by Harry Mann. The building was constructed on Powhatan Street.

One of the most exciting events of the exposition was the parade for President Theodore Roosevelt on Georgia Day, shown here assembling for the event. Harry Mann would take pictures of prominent military figures, public personalities, foreign dignitaries and royal visitors, many of whom participated in the parade.

THE PRESIDENT IN FRONT OF LIBERAL ARTS.
1430

Harry Mann photographed all of the attractions on the War Path, including the Klondike, billed as "a real trip to Alaska" and "a sight of a lifetime." The Klondike drew thousands of onlookers; it exhibited cross-country trips on dog sleds and methods used in gold mining from placer deposits.

Opposite, top: President Theodore Roosevelt's carriage was passing in front of the Manufactures and Liberal Arts Building on Georgia Day, June 10, 1907, en route to the reviewing stand when Harry Mann took this picture.

Opposite, bottom: The bridge extending over the Grand Basin was a gift from the Japanese government to the Jamestown Exposition. Japan celebrated its day at the exposition on October 2, 1907. Dr. T. Fukushima, of Tokyo Academy, told the crowd: "Fifty years ago Japan was asleep and it was the American people whose coming had found a great people and introduced them to civilization, and the friendship between the two powerful nations…will continue forever." Shortly after the Japanese attack on Pearl Harbor, December 7, 1941, the bridge was destroyed and added to the tons of riprap ringing the shoreline of Naval Air Station Norfolk.

Pharaoh's Daughter was a concession based on illusion. This War Path attraction was so successful in Hampton Roads that it was later removed from the exposition grounds and taken to London on tour.

Opposite, top: "The Battle of the *Merrimac* [*sic*] and *Monitor*" was a faithful recreation of the famous Battle of the Ironclads in Hampton Roads on March 9, 1862. This was the most successful exhibition on the War Path, though it did not open until several weeks after the exposition began. The realistic exhibits were the work of nationally known designer Edward A. Austin.

Opposite, bottom: Called "a perfect work of art" when it was finished in 1907, the Monticello Arcade was built at the south end of Monticello Avenue between City Hall Avenue and Plume Street. Designed by the firm Neff and Thompson in the Beaux-Arts style, there is nothing else like it in Virginia. But its future was not always so bright. Added to the Virginia Landmark Register on April 15, 1975, an application for the National Register of Historic Places that soon followed noted that it was "in imminent danger of demolition by the Norfolk Redevelopment and Housing Authority." Fortunately, this did not happen. It made the National Register on May 21, 1975, and has since been carefully restored. Harry Mann took this picture in 1913.

BATTLE OF THE
MERRIMAC AND MONITOR

CAFE

H.C.MANN

H.C.MANN

When President William Howard Taft came to Norfolk on November 19, 1909, to attend the Second Annual Convention of the Atlantic Deeper Waterways Commission, city fathers had public buildings dressed out in bunting and flags to greet the president. Harry C. Mann took this picture of the 1850 Norfolk City Hall and Courthouse, bedecked in patriotic bunting and lit up for the evening's passersby to admire.

Opposite, top: Harry Mann photographed the southern gable of Saint Paul's Episcopal Church from Church Street in 1908. A cannonball fired in the direction of the church on January 1, 1776, by attacking British forces under the command of John Murray, Earl of Dunmore, and later mounted to the wall of Saint Paul's that it purportedly struck, is visible at the far right, to the left of the second utility pole.

Opposite, bottom: Harry Mann took this photograph of the Norfolk benefit parade for the families of the crew of the lost USS *Nina* on June 7, 1910. The *Nina* was a United States Navy steam tugboat and the first steam-powered vessel on record to go missing in the "Devil's Triangle." It left Norfolk on March 15, 1910, bound for Havana, Cuba, to support salvage operations for the second-class battleship USS *Maine*. The *Nina* was last seen on that date just off Savannah, Georgia, steaming south. It was never seen again, and its disappearance remains one of the great mysteries of the sea. *Courtesy of the Library of Congress Prints and Photographs Division.*

The tower on the backside of Norfolk Fire Station No. 1 was used by firefighters for climbing practice. The station, located on Plume Street at the corner of Talbot Street, was photographed by Harry Mann in July 1910.

The City of Norfolk started extensive street repair, beginning with Granby Street at Queen Street (later Brambleton Avenue) and continuing to Main and Church Streets, in May 1910. The work took nearly two years. This picture shows ongoing work at the 300 block of Granby Street between Freemason Street and College Place. Most of Granby above Freemason was still residential. *Courtesy of the Sargeant Memorial Room, Norfolk Public Library.*

Construction of the U.S. Post Office and Courts Building at 235 East Plume Street began in 1899. It was designed by architects James Bosley Noel Wyatt and William G. Nolting of Baltimore, Maryland. James Knox Taylor, supervising architect of the U.S. Department of the Treasury from 1897 to 1912, who approved the plans, is listed as the architect of record. This well-preserved Classical Revival building remains one of Norfolk's most important historic structures. Harry C. Mann took his photograph of this architectural gem circa 1910. The cross street is Atlantic.

Harry Mann took this picture of the Norfolk Fire Department's Berkley Station No. 8, an engine company, circa 1913. The station was located at 311 Liberty Street.

Top: The Fosburgh Lumber Company, located on the Berkley waterfront at Walnut Street and Cummers Lane, was photographed by Harry C. Mann shortly after the death of company owner Edgar Charles Fosburgh, who died on a trip to Essex, New York, on September 10, 1910. Fosburgh and James F. Barnett founded the company in 1903; it operated from this location until 1919. Fosburgh was an officer of the Cummer Company, another Berkley lumberyard prior, from 1892 until he started his own business.

Bottom: The U.S. Navy Artificer School Headquarters at the Norfolk Navy Yard instructed ship fitters, shipwrights, blacksmiths, plumbers, fitters and painters. The sailors in this picture, taken in 1912, were culled from the fleet to attend the school. Due to the presence of several battleships at the navy yard from 1909 forward, there were four thousand or more sailors and marines in Norfolk and, at minimum, twenty-five hundred to three thousand left behind during peak deployments. This number grew exponentially over the years.

This Harry C. Mann photograph of the intersection of Granby and Tazewell Streets was taken about 1913. The Lorraine Hotel is on the corner to the right. There are many sharp, wonderful details in this picture, from D. Carpenter's Furniture Store on the corner opposite the hotel to the crisp details of cars, buggies, bicycles and sidewalk merchandise cases.

The Norfolk Police Department's first motorcycle patrol started in the Second Precinct. Two of the early Indian motorcycles shown in this 1913 Harry Mann photograph had carbon lamps for illumination, and each was equipped with rubber bullhorns. The motorcycle officers were (left to right): Patrolmen William T. Allen and Cary D. Freeman and Thomas C. Sanderlin; the fourth officer is unidentified. The sergeant standing in the precinct doorway is Seventh Sergeant John T. Godfrey. Freeman resigned from the Norfolk Police Department in 1916 with the passage of Prohibition; he went to work for the federal government's alcohol taxation unit but was later shot and killed in the line of duty by a bootlegger. The Second Precinct was located at the corner of Queen (later Brambleton Avenue) and Lincoln Streets.

Opposite, top: Harry C. Mann took this picture of the cotton wharf on Front Street about 1910. Norfolk was the fourth cotton port established in the United States.

Opposite, bottom: Norfolk Coal and Ice Company delivery drivers were photographed by Harry C. Mann in 1912 at the company's location at 225 Front Street in Norfolk's Atlantic City. The company owned several Kelly Motor Truck Company delivery trucks. This one dates to 1912. Norfolk Coal and Ice officers were Samuel B. Harrell, Joshua T. Lynch and Frank S. Sager.

(c)
H.C.MANN

NORFOLK COAL & ICE COMPANY
391-6124. 225 FRONT ST.
VIRGINIA
1
H.C.MANN

H.C. MANN

H.C. MANN

The 1858 United States Customhouse was designed by architect Ammi B. Young (1798–1874), who was then the supervising architect of the Department of the Treasury. The site was selected in 1852 on the south side of the western end of Main Street at the head of Granby Street. The contract was let in 1853, and the new building opened in December 1857 with a post office on the ground level and the customhouse operation on the floors above. Harry Mann took this picture from the foot of Granby Street, circa 1917.

Opposite, top: Harry C. Mann took this picture of yachts and sailboats anchored in Smith's Creek, a portion of which was renamed The Hague, circa 1915. Christ Episcopal Church, later Christ and Saint Luke's Episcopal Church, is on the left. Ghent's Fairfax and Pembroke Avenues (left to right) terminate on Mowbray Arch.

Opposite, bottom: French blue jackets marched down Norfolk's Main Street in the city's May 30, 1917 Memorial Day parade. Harry Mann took the picture from the south side of the street. Miller, Rhoads & Swartz Department Store at 192–202 Main Street is visible on the north side (center) near Granby. *Courtesy of the Library of Congress Prints and Photographs Division.*

East Main Street near Commerce Street on a warm summer's day in 1918 was filled with jitney buses overflowing with sailors and pedestrians too hot to continue on foot. Notably, Harry Mann caught the United States Marine Corps Recruiting Station (right); this was before the Armistice ending World War I.

Chinese immigrant George Wong opened a three-story storefront at 722–724 East Main Street called Quong Wo Yuen Company; the store first appears in the city directory in 1903. The first-floor storefront sold mostly Chinese goods, but through a side door that led to the second floor, Wong maintained offices and family living quarters. The third floor was set off for Chinese communal living; those who lived there were Chinese immigrants who needed a place to live close to work. Wong also maintained a gambling room in the back of the store for Chinese nightly socials. He married Toy Lin on March 14, 1908, in Emmanuel Church, Baltimore, Maryland, and brought her back to Norfolk, where the couple started Norfolk's first Chinese family. George and Toy Lin Wong are pictured with their children (except Lucy), circa 1919. *From left to right*: Harry, Raymond (their first born), Estelle (in her mother's lap), Alfred (on his father's lap), Lily and Annie. The Wongs returned to their native Tai-shan, China, in 1922 for their children to receive Chinese acculturation and education, which was common practice for affluent families at that time. Later, after George became ill, he gave up his Norfolk business and returned to China. *Courtesy of Art Chin.*

Opposite, bottom: Harry C. Mann took this picture, circa 1920, of an M.T. Blassingham Company lumber truck parked in front of Norfolk and Western passenger cars at Union Station, located at the foot of East Main Street. Blassingham provided lumber and railroad ties from the company's assembling yards at Twenty-sixth Street and Myers Avenue in Norfolk. Melvin T. Blassingham, owner of the company, sits at the wheel of one of his fleet of Sterling Motor Truck Company trucks. Blassingham was a longtime Norfolk civic leader whose community contributions were many, including his lifetime of involvement in the Norfolk Kiwanis, Khedive Temple, Community Fund, Norfolk General Hospital, the Salvation Army, Navy Young Men's Christian Association (YMCA) and Park Place United Methodist Church. Blassingham was a thirty-second-degree Mason. He was also known as "the father of the Oyster Bowl," an annual football game he organized with fellow Shriner and Portsmouth native Bill Kaufman to raise money for the Shriners Hospital. The first game was played in 1946. He was named First Citizen of Norfolk in 1948, and a few months later, in July 1949, he was appointed as a commissioner of the Norfolk Redevelopment and Housing Authority. Melvin and Mattie Hoy Blassingham made their home at 5421 Powhatan Avenue in Norfolk's Edgewater.

STREETS THAT MADE A TOWN

Established as a town by the Virginia General Assembly's Act for Cohabitation and Encouragement of Trade and Manufacture in 1680, Norfolk was a fifty-acre site in Lower Norfolk County on Nicholas Wise's land, a narrow, irregular peninsula between the Eastern Branch and main stem of the Elizabeth River and Town Back and Dun-in-the-Mire Creeks. John Ferebee completed his initial survey of the town's boundaries on October 19, 1680. A year to the day later, in 1681, surveyor Ferebee received payment as clerk of the militia for the purpose of "laying out the streets of the Towne." Though clearly the town of Norfolk was established by law in 1680, was surveyed almost immediately thereafter and was ready for occupation before the end of 1681, it is noteworthy that the modern city seal inexplicably bears the date of 1682 as the date when Norfolk came into existence.

In the fall of 1681, Ferebee mapped a main street for Norfolk, but also "the street that leadeth down to the waterside," later known by other names—Market Square, the Parade and Commercial Place. He also laid out "the street that leadeth to the publique spring," later Metcalf Lane; a small street north of East Main Street, later East and Bermuda Streets; and "the road that leadeth into the woods," which soon became known as Church Street.

Church Street's distance from the water's edge, East Main Street and the heart of Norfolk's commercial core was nothing more than a short-walk's distance when Ferebee first laid it out, but that would change as the town grew, and the street with it. Norfolk went from a borough in 1736 to a city in 1845. Streets remained narrow in width, much the same as Ferebee had mapped them, due to prevailing ideas rooted in ancient times when cities had walls around them, and since it cost more money to build and maintain a wall around a town, the widths of streets remained narrow, even into the nineteenth and early twentieth centuries.

The first residential expansion within the fifty acres had occurred when Colonel Samuel Boush started subdividing land along the northwest side of its main thoroughfare, then Church Street, and went northeasterly from the churchyard at Saint Paul's Episcopal Church to a point just beyond the Town Bridge, near the corner of present-day Charlotte Street. This important street, home to the city's first church and common school, first appeared on a deed dated 1737, preceding construction of the present Saint Paul's by only two years. Traveling over the ruts of this unpaved route were the carts of farmers headed to Market Square. Church Street was the only access road in and out of town to outlying plantations and simple farms.

By 1806, the Norfolk City Directory listed Church Street as "still the only avenue the town may be entered by vehicles." Described as a "noisy, busy thoroughfare" in early newspapers, Church Street was choked with stores and tenements. At the southern end of it were dry goods and grocery stores, shoe shops and ship chandlers, but northward were the homes of middle-class tailors, cabinetmakers, sea captains, blacksmiths, plasterers and butchers. Saint Paul's stood gracefully at the corner of Church and Cove Streets, and across the street was Norfolk Academy and a new Episcopal church. Church Street, though then unpaved and never in good condition, was muddy in the winter and dusty in summer but always crowded with horses, carriages, phaetons, carts and drays.

Norfolk's principal streets were paved by 1818, and after this was done, most took on the appearance of delightful promenades. The cornerstone of teh town's first customhouse was laid on April 2, 1819, an event attended by President James Monroe, Secretary of War John C. Calhoun and Navy Commodore Stephen Decatur. This customhouse, located at the corner of Widewater (later Water) and Church Streets, burned down in May 1861 during the Confederate retreat from the city.

Church and Main Streets were not the only roads to make a town. Granby Street—named in the 1760s for John Manners, Marquis of Granby, a popular eighteenth-century British general known as a spendthrift and a particularly hard drinker—set a course to become the city's most prosperous street from the moment of its humble beginnings. Gershom Nimmo, surveyor for Lower Norfolk County, laid out the original four blocks of Granby Street for Samuel Boush III, who inherited the expansive Boush tract north of Town Back Creek from his grandfather. He likely never foresaw that Granby Street would one day extend from the Elizabeth River to the Chesapeake Bay, thus becoming the longest continuous road in the city of Norfolk. Granby Street, part of Norfolk's first major real estate boom prior to the Revolutionary War, originally started on the north shore of Town Back Creek, where the F.S. Royster Building stands today, and trailed off into the woods north of Bute Street, an area later known as "The Fields." The lower part of present-day Granby Street, then known by the name Concord Street, began at Main Street and extended only two blocks north to the southern shore of Town Back Creek. Concord enjoined Granby on the other side by a stone bridge, sometimes called the "hump back" bridge. This stone bridge was Norfolk's social arbiter well into the nineteenth century, as no man who considered himself a gentleman dared cross it on his way downtown until after nine o'clock in the morning, otherwise he was stigmatized by the gentry as a member of the working class living on the wrong side of the bridge.

By the middle of the nineteenth century Norfolk had eighty-four streets and nearly fifty lanes. Most of the city's streets ran on a grid of north–south and east–west, with very few streets running at off angles from the traditional grid. Still, many streets had not been opened at this time. There were plans to open a street from the eastern end of Liberty Street to the western end of Moseley at Church to establish another direct road through the city from west to east. Plans were also made for a street east of Church near Nicholson. The names of many streets near Church were changed between 1811 and 1851. Some streets named before the Revolutionary War that bore the names of English nobles and royal family members who fell out of public favor at that time were changed for patriotic reasons. Wood Street, for example, had been George Street. There were a host of other street names that summoned the affection of Norfolk residents for a well-liked mayor, political figure or member of the Virginia gentry. Others held on to their pre–Revolutionary War names; Granby Street was one of them.

Until the early twentieth century, when commerce breached Granby Street's southern boundary with the stone bridge, it was lined with stately old Federal and Greek Revival brick and clapboard houses occupied by Norfolk's upper class. Among them were the Hardy, Newton, Taylor, Dickson and Tazewell mansions and, of course, the centuries-old "Wishing Oak," which occupied much of the Granby Street side of the Tazewell property. Under the branches of this talisman of good luck, Norfolk's lovers purportedly plighted their troth for years. But they only had a short time after the turn of the twentieth century to whisper their hearts' desire: the Wishing Oak was cut down in 1901 in the name of progress.

Possibly the oldest existing photograph of Norfolk, dating to 1865, it was taken from the top of a building near the corner of Bank and Main Streets. The street running up the center of the picture is part of Bank Street between Main and what later became City Hall Avenue but was then Town Back Creek, an area gradually filled in after the Civil War. The Merchants' and Mechanics' Bank, chartered in 1849, is in the foreground. A squad of Federal troops can be seen at the bottom of the picture, marching up Bank Street toward the creek.

Opposite, top: Running south from Main Street to the bank of the Elizabeth River, this area soon became known as Market Square, later Commercial Place, and is shown here circa 1885 looking north from Water Street. Buildings visible in the picture's center were on Main Street.

Opposite, middle: Homes and commercial buildings still shared the streets of downtown Norfolk when this photograph of Granby Street was taken circa 1902. The Granby Family Theatre is at left (foreground), and the Tazewell Building (still standing) is on the right. The backside of the Monticello Hotel is the tall structure (left) beyond the theatre. Brooke Avenue is the first street (right) beyond the cart and horse.

Opposite, bottom: An electric trolley slowly makes its way along an old downtown Norfolk street in 1903. The City of Norfolk introduced its first electric trolley in 1894, shortly after Richmond, Virginia, made history with the first electric-powered streetcar line in 1888. Within ten years of introduction, Norfolk's electric trolleys linked the city center with Sewell's Point, Ocean View, South Norfolk, Berkley, Portsmouth and Pinner's Point.

Saint John A. M. E. Church, Norfolk, Va.
General Conference A. M. E. Church, May 4-25, 1903

Above: James G. Gill (standing far right) posed with his family outside the Gill home at 257 Holt Street in 1897. Gill was in the European tea and foods business when he decided to sell coffee in 1902; thus began James G. Gill Company, coffee roasters, of Norfolk. First Colony Coffee and Tea Company evolved from Gill's company in 1970, when his great-grandsons, Thomas Jordan Brockenbrough and James Gill Brockenbrough Jr., bought the company.

Left: Saint John African American Episcopal (AME) Church is pictured here during the General Conference AME Church, May 4–25, 1903. Built between 1887 and 1888 at 539–545 East Bute Street, this is the only brick church in Norfolk that retains its distinctive northern Italian Romanesque idiom typical of Henry Hobson Richardson, a style dominant in American ecclesiastical architecture at the end of the nineteenth century. Saint John is also the last church building directly associated with Charles M. Cassell, one of Norfolk's leading late nineteenth- to early twentieth-century architects. This was the largest church built for African Americans in Norfolk in the nineteenth century.

Top: The last of Town Back Creek, which at one time extended nearly all the way to Church Street, now Saint Paul's Boulevard, was first platted in 1680. By 1880, the name City Hall Avenue had been affixed to the land that was filled-in marshland. The last of the creek, shown here, extended from Granby Street to what is today Boush Street. This picture was taken from the Norfolk and Western Railway trestle looking east. The creek was entirely filled in by 1905, and Boush Street extended up to Main Street. The buildings in the picture include the City Market and Armory Buildings (left); the 1850 city hall and courthouse (center); and the Haddington Building (right).

Bottom: Allen A. McCullough's Wharf, also called McCullough's Dock, was located at the terminus of City Hall Avenue and Boush Street. This picture, taken in 1895, shows a boat slip (foreground), all that was left of Town Back Creek. Gammage and Waller, a building supply company, is at left, and McCullough Lumber Company is at right. The trestle bridge connected Boush Street to Newton Street, later Boush Street Extended.

The six-story Haddington Building was built at the corner of Granby Street and City Hall Avenue in 1890 as one of Norfolk's first high-rise office buildings. When the Monticello Hotel, across the street, caught fire on January 1, 1918, another blaze was discovered in a Haddington elevator, prompting speculation that both fires were the work of vengeful German saboteurs. The United States entered World War I on April 6, 1917. This picture was taken about 1905.

Opposite, bottom: Photographer Harry C. Mann captured the hustle and bustle of Main Street looking west from Church Street in 1911.

Harry Mann took this photograph of Church Street looking north from East Main Street in 1910. The building rising tall above the streetcar is the L. Snyder Department Store, adapted from the old Odd Fellows Hall and Church Street Opera House. At left foreground is J.B. Bennett & Company, a jewelry store at 158 Church Street. Saint Paul's Episcopal Church is hidden in the mass of trees down the street.

Norfolk Fire Station No. 6 was built at the corner of Twelfth Street and Monticello Avenue in 1911. The seventy-foot tower was constructed for the purpose of drying hoses and conducting fire drills. This Harry Mann photograph was taken circa 1915. Of note is the motor-driven fire apparatus out front. The Norfolk Fire Department bought its first motorized vehicle—a car for the chief—in 1911. The following year, the department purchased a motor tractor, its first firefighting equipment not drawn by horses.

This view of West Freemason Street was taken by Harry Mann and made into a postcard that was mailed on January 6, 1911. In 1904, with the help of a $50,000 grant from Andrew Carnegie, Norfolk's first free public library opened on West Freemason Street, on a site donated by the children of William Selden. The library is the white columned building (center) in the picture.

Joseph M. Fentress, proprietor of the Montauk Company at 275 Granby Street, posed outside his storefront for Harry Mann in 1909. The Montauk Company manufactured ice cream. Fentress advertised his company in many publications of the period. Montauk shipped ice cream to order, in and out of town.

Taken from the intersection of Atlantic Street and City Hall Avenue looking west during the peak of summer 1910, this Harry C. Mann photograph is bustling with activity and important buildings. Starting with the right foreground is the foot of old Brewer Street. The Norfolk Armory is on the corner, and beyond the armory is the Monticello Hotel, built by David B. Lowenberg and operated by him until Colonel Charles H. Consolvo acquired it in 1905. Granby Street runs between the hotel and the Norfolk Builders' Exchange; the sign atop the exchange reads "Take a Trip to Ocean View." Along the left side of City

Hall Avenue, in the foreground, is the Terminal Arcade, built in 1901. Next to the arcade are the Virginia 5, 10 & 25¢ Store; Henry Seelinger's Star Hotel, opened at 39–41 City Hall Avenue in 1906; and the Monticello Arcade, finished in 1907. Next to the Monticello Arcade is Michael McKevitt's Saloon, a fine sample room and cigar store opened in 1903 at 23 City Hall Avenue, directly across the street from the Monticello Hotel. The electric streetcars shown here belonged to Norfolk Southern Railway and ran to Virginia Beach and Cape Henry, as well as to Ocean View.

Harry Mann took this picture of workers preparing an ice cream shipment at the Montauk Company in 1909.

Building supply house Frank T. Clark Company was located at 111 West Tazewell Street circa 1906, about the time that its building was completed. Norfolk Building Supplies Corporation, successor to Frank T. Clark, occupied the building circa 1915, when Harry C. Mann took this photograph. While the building had many tenants over the years, decades later it was developed into ten residential condominiums above the ground floor, with a restaurant at street level. This restoration was finished in 2001, representing the first substantive residential development east of Boush Street.

Opposite, bottom: Built in 1902 as the Virginia Bank and Trust Building, this beautifully appointed four-story, limestone-faced building still stands at the corner of Granby and Main Streets. The third Atlantic Hotel (razed in 1979) is next to the bank. This picture by Harry Mann was affixed to a postcard that was mailed on September 25, 1912.

Virginia Club,
Norfolk, Va.

This photograph of the Norfolk Builders' Exchange appeared in the December 24, 1911 *Virginian-Pilot*, in an article announcing that the buildings on the northwest corner of Granby Street and City Hall Avenue would be razed and the new twelve-story F.S. Royster Building would be built there the following year. Demolition was quick. By January 1, 1912, the first of more than seventeen hundred piles were being driven for the F.S. Royster Building. It was finished by the end of that year.

Opposite: The seven-story Virginia Club building, shown here on this 1907 postcard, opened in March 1904 on the southwest corner of Granby and Plume Streets. The club had owned another building on this site, but it burned in January 1902. New York architect Kenneth M. Murchison Jr., best known for his railroad terminals, commercial buildings, hospitals and hotels, was hired to design a new home for the city's premier gentlemen's club. This is the only such club building of its era still standing in Norfolk.

Granby Street at City Hall Avenue was photographed by Harry C. Mann a little after eleven o'clock in the morning on a warm summer's day in 1912. Take note of the plethora of parasols, the newly constructed Frank S. Royster Building at left foreground and the grand curves of the Monticello Hotel at right. Also notable is the outdoor display case at the corner entrance to the hotel.

Harry Mann took this photograph of City Hall Avenue looking west toward Granby Street about 1915. The Monticello Arcade is at left foreground, the Frank S. Royster Building at center and the Monticello Hotel at right.

Opposite, top: Photographer Lewis Wickes Hines (1874–1940) took this picture of Western Union delivery boy No. 23, Raymond Bykes, of Norfolk, Virginia, in June 1911. Hines observed of Bykes: "Said he was fourteen years old. Works until after one in the morning every night. He is precocious and not a little 'tough.' Has been here at this office for only three months, but he already knows the Red Light District thoroughly and goes there constantly. He told me he often sleeps down at the Bay Line boat docks all night. Several times I saw his mother hanging around the office, but she seemed more concerned about getting his pay envelope than anything else." Hines photographed Bykes on Granby Street. *Courtesy of the Library of Congress Prints and Photographs Division.*

Opposite, bottom: The Fox River Butter Company, located at 90 Roanoke Avenue and managed by John B. Morgan, was photographed by Harry C. Mann, circa 1910. The butter business opened at this location in 1905 and was gone by 1919.

FOX RIVER BUTTER CO.
FRESH
EGGS
"Clover Hill" Butter
FOX RIVER BUTTER CO.
CLOVER HILL BUTTER
MEADOW GOLD BUTTER

The Essex Building was built at the corner of East Plume and Bank Streets in 1907; this picture dates to that period. Among the building's occupants were the Merchant Savings and Loan, West Detective Agency, the offices of Barton Myers and, later, the Italian, British, French, Venezuelan, Argentine, Colombian and Cuban Consulates.

The Norfolk County Ferry Building at the foot of Commercial Place was photographed on April 3, 1915, after a hurricane; it was still raining when the picture was taken.

The Hotel Fairfax, located on City Hall Avenue at Randolph Street and designed by the Norfolk firm of Breese and Mitchell, was completed in April 1907 in time to play host to visitors to the Jamestown Exposition being held at Sewell's Point. Breese and Mitchell designed the Virginia House at the Jamestown Exposition. Although little is known about Charles Parker Breese, Benjamin Franklin Mitchell (1870–1956) is known to have designed a number of local landmarks, among them buildings near the Fairfax: the molasses tank that stood in Freemason on the site of the Pagoda; a part of Southgate Terminals, built between 1916 and 1917 at West Tazewell and Duke Street and now gone; and also schools, churches and houses in Norfolk. This picture of the Fairfax Hotel was taken circa 1915.

Norfolk Fire Department Ladder Truck C was covered and embedded in ice after battling the January 1, 1918 Monticello Hotel fire. The New Year's Day blaze destroyed four Granby Street buildings, killed three firemen and injured dozens more but remains best known as "the Monticello Hotel fire." Affected buildings included the Dickson Building at 226–230 Granby Street, the first to catch fire; the Monticello Hotel's northwest corner; the Lenox Building; and the D. Carpenter Building next door. Another fire started in the Granby Theatre but was quickly controlled. Since World War I was raging, local police rounded up nineteen Germans and turned them over to federal authorities as suspected arsonists.

Monticello Hotel owner Charles H. Consolvo spared no expense to rebuild it. The hotel reopened in early 1919. This is the main-floor lobby, photographed at the time of the "new" Monticello's opening. *Courtesy of the Sargeant Memorial Room, Norfolk Public Library.*

Opposite, bottom: Harry C. Mann took this picture of the Fruit Supply Company's Sterling Motor Company delivery truck in 1919. The company was located at 236 Water Street, along Norfolk's expansive downtown waterfront.

The Lorraine Hotel, located at the corner of Granby and Tazewell Streets, is pictured as it looked about 1920. The building was completed to accommodate guests for the upcoming Jamestown Exposition in 1907. Ferguson and Calrow were the architects of this once beautifully appointed seven-story hotel. While not large, the Lorraine was believed to be among the most elegant and prominent hotels of its day, boasting a fine café for ladies and gentlemen and a stag grill room known as the Lorraine Hotel Rathskeller. The charm and gentility of the old Lorraine Hotel have long since faded from Granby Street.

Opposite, top: Harry Mann stood looking east from Boush Street down City Hall Avenue. Three of the city's most distinctive buildings are in his picture: the F.S. Royster Building (left), completed in 1912 on the site of the former Builders' Exchange; the 1850 City Hall (center); and the Fairfax Hotel (right). Mann took this picture about 1915.

Opposite, bottom: Elias A. Codd's Granby Delicatessen, located at 1206 Granby Street, was celebrating Coffee Week from March 29 to April 3, 1920, when Harry Mann took this picture. Codd's store windows were filled with Queens Blend Coffee products and advertisements.

& Billiards
Sloan's
Liniment
Kills Pain
HOTEL
FAIRFAX

Coffee Week
MARCH 29TH-APRIL 3RD
GRANBY DELICATESSEN
DRINK
GOOD
COFFEE
And
LIVE
LONG
GOOD
COFFEE
Be
HAPPY
GRANBY DELICATESSEN
WE RECEIVE QUEENS BLEND COFFEE
DAY ROASTED-ALWAYS FRESH

Rice's department store was on both sides of the Norva Theatre when Charles Borjes took this picture on January 22, 1926. Located between Market and Freemason Streets, the Norva presented the best of vaudeville and first-run picture shows. The movie on the Norva's marquee is Metro-Goldwyn-Mayer's *Tower of Lies*, released on October 11, 1925, and starring Norma Shearer and Lon Chaney. *Courtesy of the Sargeant Memorial Room, Norfolk Public Libarry.*

GLORY DAYS

Gone are Norfolk's salad days, that glorious time between 1900 and the end of World War II when the city's streets teemed with people and Granby Street was at the center of it all. Crowded with well-stocked department stores, top-rated hotels and theatres, interesting eating establishments and a broad selection of specialty shops, Granby Street was well patronized and the hub of the city in every respect. "Granby Street in those days was the place to learn what was going on in the Norfolk area," *Virginian-Pilot* columnist George Tucker opined on January 19, 1986. "When I was trying to get the low down on a rumor that was going the rounds, I applied for further information to a Norfolk matron who knew something about everything afoot in the area." He was not disappointed by her reply: "I don't know anything about it right now," she told him, a twinkle in her eye, "but give me fifteen minutes on Granby Street and I'll have all of the details"—and she did.

The most frequented shops, restaurants and theatres were within the first eight blocks of Granby Street between Main Street and Brambleton Avenue. Prominent buildings between Main and Plume Streets included the imposing Ionic columns of Virginia Bank and Trust and the third Atlantic Hotel, with its two naked cupids frolicking over its main entrance. The block that followed included the Law Building, home to many of Norfolk's most prominent attorneys, and beginning at City Hall Avenue, on the west side was the F.S. Royster Building and on the east, the Monticello Hotel, owned by Colonel Charles H. Consolvo. But there was also Shulman's men's store, the Nusbaum Book and Art Company, Paul-Gale-Greenwood Jewelry Store and Nunnally's candy store. North of Tazewell Street were the Lorraine Hotel, Freeman's book and stationery store, Burrow-Martin's Pharmacy, the Oriental Chop Suey Café, Smith & Welton Department Store, Loew's and Norva Theatres, Hardy's jewelry store and the Martha Washington Candy Company.

The intersection of Granby and Freemason Streets, later dominated by the YMCA, Southland Hotel and Ames and Brownley's department store, had earlier been the site of the Leache-Wood Seminary, Granby Street Methodist Church, the Merrimack Club and a middling boardinghouse. The latter clutch of corner occupants led one Norfolk observer to declare, "By God! This is education, salvation, damnation and starvation corner!"

Farther north was the Granby Theatre, the Flatiron Building and, until it was struck by lightning on May 23, 1921, and burned down, Saint Luke's Episcopal Church at the corner of Granby and Bute Streets. Saint Luke's was considered, conservatively, one of the most beautiful churches in the South. Designed by Boston, Massachusetts architect W.P. Wentworth, one of the most unique features of the church was the antique oak used to construct its doors, wainscoting, reredos, pews and chancel furniture. The wood came from the wreck of the Norwegian bark *Dictator*, which ran aground below Virginia Beach in March 1891 on its voyage from Pensacola, Florida, to West Bartlepool, England. The congregation believed that using the wood from this fated ship in a holy place was a fitting memorial to those who lost their lives aboard it. Saint Luke's was finished on October 18, 1892.

Granby Street epitomized the joyful life that preceded the end of World War II. But the rest of downtown followed. The photographs that follow show happy, glorious times. We see a busy waterfront; commercial houses alive with shopkeepers and customers; sailors in crisp white uniforms piled into cars and headed downtown; and streets, buildings, homes, churches and people who have now faded from memory, gone with the loss of those old enough to recall them and to later generations who wanted no part of them. Taken altogether, there is much about Norfolk's past that has never been told and, certainly, has not been seen.

C.S. Measell's Fruits & Produce operated out of an open-air storefront at the City Market on Tazewell Street between Monticello Avenue and Brewer Street from 1899 to 1911. Clarence Samuel Measell, its owner, died on August 2, 1915, at age fifty-two. The Pure Food Store, the brick building at center on the corner of Washington Street (later Market Street) and Monticello Avenue, was in business from 1907 to 1910. Harry C. Mann took this picture in 1907.

Horse-and-buggies covered in sunflowers, mums and carnations were readied by their owners for the city's Memorial Day parade on May 30, 1904. Preparations took place in the vicinity of buildings fronting Granby Street (left) that include the George L. Crow Company, a purveyor, repairer and manufacturer of stoves, tin and sheet iron. Established in Norfolk in 1826, the company was originally located on Commercial Row in an area that extended from Water Street south to the river and from the east side of the Market House. The founder's son, also George L. Crow, was a master tin and coppersmith; he died on February 14, 1879. The company moved to 86 Granby Street in 1900.

Dedication of the Navy YMCA on Brooke Avenue occurred less than a month after the return of the battleship USS *Virginia* (BB-13) from its round-the-world voyage as part of the Great White Fleet, which departed Hampton Roads on December 17, 1907, and returned on February 22, 1909. The *Virginia*'s crew presented the Navy YMCA with the 615-foot silk homeward-bound pennant, which the ship's officers had made to order in China for $605 in honor of its opening. The *Virginia*'s officers and enlisted sailors also presented the Navy YMCA with $1,000 cash raised on the trip home, as well as another $450 from the battleship USS *Kentucky* (BB-6), to furnish the building.

Opposite, bottom: On June 18, 1906, it was announced that American industrialist John D. Rockefeller had given $250,000 to build a Navy YMCA in Norfolk (shown here shortly after it opened at 130 Brooke Avenue at the corner of Boush Street). Formally dedicated on March 17, 1909, with William Sloane, of New York and Norfolk presiding, it was intended to be among the finest YMCAs in the country with the most modern equipment available. The navy YMCA movement began at the end of the Spanish-American War. The first navy YMCA in the country opened in 1902 at the Brooklyn Navy Yard. In the same year, a navy YMCA was also established on Norfolk's Church Street.

The piers and warehouses of the Old Dominion Steamship Company, located at the foot of Church Street (today Saint Paul's Boulevard) and Water Street, were crowded with small general cargo vessels loaded with baskets of fresh produce from farms along the waterways of the Elizabeth River and also from northeastern North Carolina. Before the advent of interstates and the shift to tractor-trailers to ship such goods, boats were the preferred method of moving farmers' produce to the city for local sale and shipment elsewhere, usually to markets in the North. This picture was taken in 1912.

OLD DOMINION LINE.
NORFOLK.VA

The 700 block of Granby Street, between numbers 719 and 723, was populated by automobile dealers, among them C.L. Young Motor Cars, which sold Pierce Arrows, Haynes and Buick automobiles and automobile supplies. Next door, the Pope-Republic Company retailed Pope-Hartford cars and Republic tires, and Overland Cars, owned by distributor Arthur W. Depue, specialized in delivery cars, Willys delivery trucks and automobile supplies. Harry C. Mann posed in his own photograph—unusual for Mann—and is standing on the left in front of C.L. Young's, with his coat draped over his arm. The picture is circa 1910. *Courtesy of the Sargeant Memorial Room, Norfolk Public Library.*

Harry Mann took this photograph of an unidentified Norfolk office in January 1913. Catalogues for Pratt & Whitney adjustable reamers and other tools that would be used to maintain and repair automobiles sit atop the desk, perhaps offering a clue that the office belonged to someone in the auto business.

Opposite, bottom: Every one of these young boys and girls went to work when the whistle blew at noon on June 15, 1911, in the Chesapeake Knitting Mills in Berkley, Norfolk, Virginia. While some of the older boys provided their names to photographer Lewis Wickes Hines, the youngest refused to give their names, worried that he would report them to the National Child Labor Committee. Located at the corner of Twelfth and B Streets, Chesapeake Knitting Mills was originally owned by David Lowenberg; he also owned the nearby Elizabeth Knitting Mills. New York textile magnate William Sloane purchased both mills in 1903. *Courtesy of the Library of Congress Prints and Photographs Division.*

Norfolk Fire Station No. 5 was located at 733 East Main Street at Reid's Lane in 1913 when Harry Mann took this picture. The station first moved to this site in 1913.

Opposite, top: The Coburn Motor Car Company was located on Granby Street between Charlotte and Bute Streets; Bute is to the left and Charlotte to the right in this Harry Mann photograph, taken circa 1914. Owned by Timothy Gray Coburn, the dealership opened in 1910 at this location. He sold Studebakers. Coburn sponsored rising stars on the auto racing circuit as early as the year his dealership opened. Norfolk's Fairgrounds, adjacent to today's Fairmount Park, hosted automobile races as early as December 1–3, 1910, when Coburn and several cars and drivers were suspended for one year by the American Automobile Association (AAA) for holding an unsanctioned meet there. The church (left) is Saint Luke's Episcopal.

The Virginia Paper Box Company, located at Granby Street and East Twenty-second Street, was photographed by Harry C. Mann, circa 1915. The company was owned by William D. Hemingway, president; Jacob S. Heller, vice-president; and Samuel Linthicum, secretary. They opened their paper box enterprise at 301 Front Street in 1907 and moved to East Main Street, briefly, before moving to this location in 1912.

THE BYBEE SANITARIUM
NORFOLK, VA.

Photographer Frank J. Conway took this picture of the Chamber of Commerce Dining Room on the top floor—the thirteenth—of the old National Bank of Commerce Building, built in 1905 on Main Street, about 1915.

Opposite, top: William Hemingway's company was Virginia Paper Box until 1920, when the name changed to Corrugated Paper Company. The name changed again in 1923 to Carolina Paper Box Company, and the company moved to East Plume Street. The company closed in 1929, largely due to the deaths of two principals—Hemingway on May 20, 1929, and Heller on August 28, 1929. Harry Mann photographed the officers and clerks of the Virginia Paper Box Company circa 1915.

Opposite, bottom: The Bybee Sanitarium, pictured on this circa 1915 postcard, was located at 631 Westover Avenue in Norfolk's Ghent. Dr. Harry Rainey Bybee, a doctor of chiropractic, quartered his patients here from 1911 to 1923, when Cox Funeral Home occupied the site. Dr. Bybee was a distinguished member of his profession, attaining national acclaim as president of the National and Virginia Chiropractic Associations and for his client list. Among those who sought treatment from Dr. Bybee were Billy Sunday, General John J. Pershing, Frank Sinatra, World Series winning manager Billy Southworth, Yankees shortstop Phil Rizzuto and Al Jolson. Dr. Bybee practiced chiropractic medicine in Norfolk for forty-one years; his last office was located in the New Monroe Building. Born on February 18, 1891, in Lancaster, Ohio, the son of a chiropractor, Dr. Bybee died on April 4, 1952, at his home at 730 Westover Avenue.

A 1913 nor'easter flooded City Hall Avenue looking west toward Granby Street. The Monticello Hotel is on the right, and the F.S Royster Building is at center. City Hall Avenue had originally been a creek bed when Norfolk was laid out in 1680; thus, it was susceptible to nature taking back that which was hers. *Courtesy of Carroll H. Walker.*

Harry Mann took this picture looking south on Granby Street from Tazewell Street in the summer of 1918. United States Navy sailors choke the streets. It is World War I, and they make up the majority of Norfolk's street crowd. Eight of the eleven automobiles in the street have signs on the windshield offering rides to particular destinations. These vehicles were called jitney buses; it cost five cents, or "a jitney," to ride in one of them. The Dickson Building is at left foreground.

Opposite, top: The old Berkley Bridge extended from the foot of East Main Street to South Main Street in Berkley. Harry C. Mann took this picture from Norfolk looking toward Berkley just after the bridge was built in August 1916. The bridge was a privately owned toll bridge that cost travelers two cents to cross. The City of Norfolk acquired the bridge in 1946 and took it down in 1952 after constructing a larger structure. At the far end of the bridge (left) is Riveredge, built about 1728 by John Herbert and, later, the home of Mary Pinckney Hardy, mother of General Douglas A. MacArthur.

Opposite, bottom: Garrett and Company, makers of Virginia Dare wines, popular in the early 1900s, was located at the foot of Chestnut Street in Norfolk's Berkley. The wine company began operations in 1903 and continued until 1916, when Virginia Prohibition took effect that November. The mansion (right) was the residence of Paul Garrett, president of the company. The photograph was taken by Harry C. Mann in 1915.

A sea of U.S. Navy sailors paraded down Granby Street as far as the eye could see on August 30, 1923, in celebration of the national encampment of the Veterans of Foreign Wars (VFW) in Norfolk. It was during the 1923 campaign that the VFW evolved the idea, which resulted in the VFW Buddy Poppy fashioned by disabled and needy veterans who were paid for their work as a practical means of providing assistance for these comrades. This plan was formally presented for adoption to the 1923 encampment of the VFW at Norfolk. It passed. *Courtesy of the Sargeant Memorial Room, Norfolk Public Library.*

Norfolk Naval Station Building 101, photographed by Harry C. Mann, remained an integral part of the modern-day Naval Supply Center for decades. Known as the "Biggest Store in the World," this building was formally commissioned on March 1, 1919, about the time Mann took this picture. There were only a few permanent warehouses and a handful of temporary structures in the base's supply network at that time. The history of the Naval Supply Center began on October 11, 1917, when Building 100 was completed.

Opposite, top: As World War I drew to a close, city business and community leaders established an executive committee to decide how to best memorialize Norfolk's fallen. The Memorial Campaign Steering Committee, photographed on March 17, 1919, consisted of (left to right): William Williams Robertson, Henry Graham Barbee, Alexander Pinkham Grice, Moe Levy and Richard Latimer Dobie. Robertson was an officer of the U.S. Shipping Board, Division of Operations, with offices in the Monroe Building. Barbee was the owner of a wholesale confectionary on Tazewell Street that bore his family name. Grice was president of the Guaranty Title and Trust Corporation in the Law Building. Levy was a lawyer with an office in the National Bank of Commerce Building, and Dobie was an agent for the Atlantic Life Insurance Company.

The 723-foot steamship SS *George Washington* was Norddeutscher German Lloyd Shipping Company's largest pre–World War I ship. Launched on June 12, 1909, the *George Washington* was designed to carry 2,679 passengers, half in steerage. It made monthly runs from Europe to the United States until the start of World War I in August 1914. Caught at its berth at Hoboken, New Jersey, just across the Hudson River from New York City, it stayed put until the United States entered the war in early April 1917. The *George Washington* was seized by the United States and converted to a troop transport. It even played an important role in postwar diplomatic efforts, twice carrying President Woodrow Wilson to France for prolonged negotiations resulting in the Treaty of Versailles. After decommissioning by the War Department in 1921, it returned to commercial service as an American-flagged ocean liner of the United States Line by the same name. Ten years later, it was mothballed. Briefly pressed into wartime service in 1941 as the USS *Catlin* (AP-19), the War Department ultimately transferred it to civilian operators in the United States and Great Britain as the transport *George Washington* from the end of 1941 into 1942. Fitted with new oil-fired boilers to improve the ship's performance, from April 1943 to a period just after the war's end, it was again an army transport. The SS *George Washington* was scrapped in 1951. When this photograph of the SS *George Washington* was taken in 1925, it had just moved out of its repair berth at Norfolk Navy Yard into the main stem of the Elizabeth River at Norfolk's Town Point.

Dating photographs often comes down to something as simple as what was playing at the movie houses. Hollywood studios released two movies simultaneously on November 28, 1931: *The Cheat* starting Tallulah Bankhead, which was playing at the Loew's Theatre, and *Corsair*, starring Chester Morris, showing at the Norva (foreground). Charles Borjes took this picture of the 300 block of Granby Street between Market and Freemason Streets around the release date of these two movies debuting at the Loew's and Norva. Loew's left Granby Street in October 1979. *Courtesy of the Sargeant Memorial Room, Norfolk Public Library.*

Coca-Cola
GRANBY
LOEW'S STATE
MARION DAVIES
CLARK GABLE

NEWPORT THEATRE
ENTIRE WEEK
MONDAY 14
Chrysler SERVICE

The cornerstone of the federal courthouse and post office at the 600 block of Granby Street was laid on September 7, 1933. Charles Borjes was dispatched to take photographs of the event, which drew hundreds of dignitaries, community leaders and curious citizens. *Courtesy of the Sargeant Memorial Room, Norfolk Public Library.*

Opposite, top: Several years later, Charles Borjes took this picture of the 300 block of Granby Street, with the Loew's Theatre (right) and Hardy's Jewelers, Martha Washington Candy Company and the imposing Southland Hotel (left) in the foreground. The photograph is dated by the Loew's marquee. The Loew's had just debuted Marion Davies and Clark Gable in *Cain and Mabel*, released on September 26, 1936. *Courtesy of the Sargeant Memorial Room, Norfolk Public Library.*

Opposite, bottom: The future site of Norfolk's federal courthouse and post office at the 600 block of Granby Street, looking north toward Queen Street (not yet Brambleton Avenue), was photographed by Charles S. Borjes on March 14, 1932. The large tank structures in the background are the gasworks up on Monticello Avenue adjacent to Cedar Grove Cemetery. *Courtesy of the Sargeant Memorial Room, Norfolk Public Library.*

Charles Borjes took this picture of Boy Scouts marching in the May 30, 1932 Memorial Day parade down Granby Street. The scouts are passing the former Norfolk College for Young Ladies (right foreground), then the Hotel Lee, on the northwest corner of Granby Street and College Place. The Oriental Chop Suey Café, on the southwest corner, occupied the building originally known as the home of the turn-of-the-twentieth-century Burk-Hume Piano Company, a pioneer in the marketing of phonographs and 78 rpm records. *Courtesy of the Sargeant Memorial Room, Norfolk Public Library.*

CHOP SUEY
AFE
ORIENTAL
HOTEL
LEE
$1 00 UP
PEOPLES
BOYS
WOMEN
CHILDREN
WASHINGTON
HOTEL LEE
HOTEL LE

Streetcars slipped off their tracks at Monticello Avenue and Charlotte Street, derailed by excessive snow, on February 7, 1936. This was a memorable day for city travelers. Streetcar service was suspended as icy winds whipped through Norfolk streets and brought the city to a standstill. *Courtesy of the Sargeant Memorial Room, Norfolk Public Library.*

Opposite, top: H.D. Vollmer took this picture of baseball legend Babe Ruth (center) at the Washington Boat Docks, located at the foot of Colley Avenue and Front Street, in the summer of 1934. Only a few of the children around Ruth are identifiable: J.C. Larkin (left foreground in the white shirt, hands on his hips); H.D. Vollmer Jr. and his sister, Clara Vollmer (standing just to the right of Larkin); David Costas (standing directly next to Ruth); and Woodie Kite (wearing the sailor's hat next to Ruth). *Courtesy of Clara J. Vollmer.*

Opposite, bottom: H.D. Vollmer photographed the Wood Towing Company tug *Atlas* as it passed under the old Berkley Bridge in 1935.

CORNER

Photographer Carroll Herbert Walker took this picture of City Hall Avenue from the fourth floor of the F.S. Royster Building in September 1939 at the beginning of a nor'easter. By day's end, the street, once a creek extending nearly all the way to Church Street, flooded quickly, becoming impassable to automobiles, streetcars and pedestrians.

Opposite, top: The last of America's glory-seeking aviators, Douglas "Wrong Way" Corrigan earned his nickname with his wrong-way flight from New York to Dublin, Ireland, on July 17, 1938, in a rebuilt Curtiss J-1 Robin that he had bought from a salvage yard for $310. Just weeks after this flight, on August 30, 1938, Corrigan arrived in town via the Glenrock Airport; he was honored with a parade, a key to the city and dinner. Corrigan (center in the leather flight jacket) is seated to the left of Norfolk mayor John A. Gurkin.

Opposite, bottom: Charles Borjes took this picture of Church Street looking north from East Main Street on November 21, 1938. While mainstays like Matthew Tavss's children's clothier, L. Snyder Department Store and Altschul's were still there, most of Church Street's favorite establishments were already gone, some driven away with the closure of key thoroughfares—the price of progress. The mass of trees (left) in the background of the picture marks the location of Saint Paul's Episcopal Church. *Courtesy of the Sargeant Memorial Room, Norfolk Public Library.*

Norfolk's first blackout of World War II happened on the night of December 13, 1941. Civilian defense authorities executed the blackout without warning to test the public's responsiveness. The police department's only complaint was that there were too many cars on a Saturday night trying to operate with dimmed lights on darkened streets, a situation that led to a few mishaps, none serious. Charles Borjes took this picture. *Courtesy of the Sargeant Memorial Room, Norfolk Public Library.*

JACKASS MAIL
WALLY BEERY
MARJORIE MAIN

NAVY
RECRUITIN
SERVICE
SEPTEMBER

Looking south from the west side of Granby Street, Charles Borjes took this picture of passersby, many of them U.S. Navy sailors in their whites, moving past Smith & Welton Department Store on August 16, 1945. Smith & Welton, opened in 1898 at the corner of Granby and Market Streets, was Norfolk's leading and last remaining downtown department store before it closed in 1988. Sailors standing on the street across from Smith & Welton are waiting at the foot of College Place for a ride back to Naval Station Norfolk, which loaded cars at that corner. *Courtesy of the Sargeant Memorial Room, Norfolk Public Library.*

Opposite, top: Members of the Naval Air Station Norfolk swing band entertained throngs of passersby on Granby Street on July 17, 1942, during a wartime bond rally. Charles S. Borjes took this picture, one of several of this event. *Courtesy of the Sargeant Memorial Room, Norfolk Public Library.*

Opposite, bottom: Future Hall of Fame New York Yankees' shortstop Phil Rizzuto joined the U.S. Navy on September 8, 1942, in Norfolk, a moment captured for posterity by *Ledger-Dispatch* photographer H.D. Vollmer. Rizzuto was named an all-star and went to the World Series that year. He served three years in the navy during World War II. *Courtesy of the Sargeant Memorial Room, Norfolk Public Library.*

Top: Norfolk's Armistice Day was celebrated on Monday, November 12, 1945. Crowds, seven deep to the curb on both sides of Granby Street, watched and cheered the city's largest assembly of military units to ever participate in a parade in Hampton Roads. *Courtesy of the Sargeant Memorial Room, Norfolk Public Library.*

Bottom: In the aftermath of Norfolk's Armistice Day parade on November 12, 1945, hordes of onlookers filled Granby Street. *Courtesy of the Sargeant Memorial Room, Norfolk Public Library.*

GONE FOREVER

"Gone forever" is a final nod to beloved places that remind us of our past, most known only in the photographs that follow and in the memories of those old enough to remember them. The pictures that follow speak for themselves. There is the lovely French's Hotel, which played host to heads of state, military heroes, poets and pundits and presidents of the United States. There is the home of George Newton, former mayor of Norfolk; the S.A. Stevens Furniture Company, the only remaining Second Empire building standing in downtown Norfolk until it was razed in 2007; and the Atlantic Hotel, the third by that name, which succumbed to a later phase of urban redevelopment that took down more downtown landmarks in the 1970s and 1980s. There are many more commercial storefronts that have retreated with the passage of time.

Some of the places now gone were missed long ago, when the march of progress removed them from the Norfolk scene. An article in the October 12, 1925 *Virginian-Pilot* and *Norfolk Landmark* made the early observation that Norfolk's stately Colonial homes were "vanishing under the major touch of progressive business along Granby Street," the city's premier retail and entertainment district. The march of progress in the city's retail hub has been advancing north up Granby Street since 1900, "brushing old historic homesteads into the discard to make room for modern stores and office buildings," many of which have since succumbed to later generations' ideas of "progress." Progress has not been overly kind to Norfolk's historically and architecturally significant buildings.

French's Hotel (left foreground), looking west from Church and East Main Streets, opened on April 19, 1837. Its first guest was France's Prince Charles Louis Napoleon Bonaparte, who returned home from exile as Emperor Louis Napoleon in 1852. French's became the National Hotel in 1846, and on August 25, 1860, Stephen A. Douglass made a speech from its balcony. Named Purcell House from 1881 to 1897, it became Hotel Norfolk from 1897 to 1900. John Willis Jr. Furniture moved into the building in 1901; by then it was called the Eclipse Building. A succession of furniture businesses followed, including Willis-Smith-Crall from 1906 to 1913; Forrest-Hall Furniture, 1914; Norfolk Furniture Manufacturing Company, 1915; and Forrest Furniture, 1916. Many tenants and periods of vacancy would follow. French's was razed by Norfolk Redevelopment and Housing Authority in 1961, and with it went the place that had welcomed a cross-section of American history, from an emperor, Presidents of the United States John Tyler and Grover Cleveland to General Winfield Scott and Mark Twain.

Opposite, top: The home of George Newton, which stood on the southwest corner of College Place and Granby Street, was built on what had been part of the original estate of Samuel Boush. The land was conveyed in 1801 by Conway Whittle to Thomas Willing, who subsequently sold the lot for one dollar to the Bank of the United States at Norfolk, which Willing represented, on March 25, 1802. Construction was begun almost immediately, and on September 7, 1803, the bank opened for business in the building. This was Norfolk's first and only bank at that time. Two brick guardhouses for bank sentries were also built on either side of the front entrance (these are visible in the photograph). The bank closed in 1811. George Newton, from a leading Norfolk family and a former mayor of the borough, did not purchase the property until 1826. The property remained in the Newton family until 1893, when it was sold to Charles Wesley Fentress for commercial purposes. This picture was taken in 1883.

Harry Mann's photograph of the George Newton home appeared in the July 10, 1910 *Virginian-Pilot*, which announced that the house would soon be razed.

Built in 1869 and first occupied by the S.A. Stevens Furniture Company, this Second Empire building at 100–102 East Main Street is no longer standing, demolished in August 2007 to make way for a hotel convention center. Massachusetts natives Samuel A. Stevens and James S. Ames sold furniture, pianos and organs there until 1896, when both returned to their home state. Watt, Rettew and Clay occupied the building from 1896 to 1929; owners David F. Watt, William M. Rettew and Alfred Clay closed the Norfolk store after the stock market crash. The storefront was vacant until 1937, starting a succession of occupants selling furniture until 1975, when it was renovated and subdivided into office and retail space. Charles Borjes took this picture in 1930.

Opposite, bottom: Ohef Sholom Temple was established in 1844 and remains the largest and oldest Jewish reform congregation in Hampton Roads. The synagogue building shown here was built at the corner of East Freemason Street and Monticello Avenue. It was dedicated on May 23, 1902, about the time this picture was taken, and there it remained until it was destroyed by fire on February 12, 1916. Temple was held temporarily at the Ghent Club on Olney Road across Smith's Creek form Mowbray Arch until land on Stockley Gardens at Raleigh Avenue was acquired and a new building finished in 1918.

The foundation of the second Atlantic Hotel (shown here) was laid in August 1867. Located at Main and Granby Streets, the new Atlantic Hotel was several blocks over from the first hotel by this name that had been destroyed earlier that year by fire. The first hotel had been situated at Main and Gray (later Atlantic) Streets. Like its predecessor, the second Atlantic Hotel burned to the ground on January 31, 1902; it was replaced by a third Atlantic Hotel on the same site. This picture (of the second Atlantic) was taken in 1896.

The cornerstone of the City Market and Armory was laid on October 28, 1890. The *Public Ledger* called it "one of the epochs in the city's history." Shown here circa 1905, the market was the place to which farmers from all over southeastern Virginia and northeastern North Carolina brought their fresh produce, meats and seafood and canned, cured and baked goods. It was torn down in 1955.

CITY MARKET
BICYCLES
REPAIRING

A vacant storefront at the corner of Fenchurch and East Main Streets served as a polling place for a primary election day on October 13, 1903. The man holding the cane (right) is identified as John M. Arnold, an attorney who started out in the Norfolk city attorney's office and later became the Norfolk commonwealth attorney.

This E.F. Jakeman Jewelry Store postcard was printed in 1905, the same year Edward Francis Jakeman opened his own shop on East Main Street between Bank and Commercial Place. Jakeman's reputation as a master watchmaker and jeweler was well known. He had partnered with William H. Chapman from 1893 as Chapman and Jakeman. Jakeman sold watches, diamonds, jewelry and silver; his shop was an East Main Street mainstay until 1923, when Jakeman moved to 335 Granby Street. He retired in 1929.

Lewis Wickes Hines took this picture of Dominick, a young Norfolk newsboy, in June 1911. Dominick, last name unknown, was selling the *Ledger-Dispatch* for the Norfolk Newspapers. Hines was photographing children working street trades for the National Child Labor Committee. He observed many small boys selling newspapers throughout Virginia but noted that the number in Norfolk was especially high. *Courtesy of the Library of Congress Prints and Photographs Division.*

CASH
PRIZES
ALSO
$117.00
ABSOLU
FOR FUL
SEE LEDG
CALL 3
ARTHUR
355
PRIZES
PAUL GALE GREEN
JOHN L.
ULLIVAN
HAMPION of CHAMPIONS
MANAGEMENT FRANK HALL
ADEMY OF MUSIC
WEEK COMMENCING MONDAY JUNE 12

N-GERA BOTTLING CO.
THE GIN-GERA COMPANY INC.
856
854
OFFICE
ENTRANCE
Gin-Gera 5¢
"IT GINGERS YOU UP"

National Laundry operated at 404–406 Twenty-second Street from 1920, the year Harry C. Mann took this picture of company officers and employees with their trucks and a lone buggy. National Laundry's tenure in Norfolk was brief; it was gone by 1927.

Opposite, top: These Norfolk newsboys were photographed by Lewis Hines in front of the Van Wyck Academy of Music on East Main Street (where the Selden Arcade stands today) in June 1911. The last of the bare-knuckle fighters, heavyweight boxing great John L. Sullivan was set to make a celebrity appearance there starting Monday, June 12. A large poster advertising the event is pasted to the building behind them. Sullivan was far too old to box by then. The boys are holding copies of the *Ledger-Dispatch*. *Courtesy of the Library of Congress Prints and Photographs Division.*

Opposite, bottom: Norfolk was home to an often forgotten enterprise of the early twentieth century: the bottling industry. Norfolk could claim one indigenous soft drink company, Gin-Gera Company, which bottled and sold a soda drink similar to ginger ale. Located at 852–856 Granby Street, Gin-Gera Company predated both Coca-Cola and Pepsi Cola, which came to the city in 1902 and 1912, respectively, and remained an innovator in the bottling business until the end of World War I, when Gin-Gera ceased production of its delectable ginger sweet water. Harry C. Mann took this picture of the Gin-Gera Company, circa 1917. *Courtesy of the Sargeant Memorial Room, Norfolk Public Library.*

As a navy town, Norfolk has had its share of great ships call it home. Members of the highly decorated crew of the USS *Utah* (BB-31) had their picture taken at the No. 1 gun turret in the summer of 1914, after returning from action at Vera Cruz that spring. During action at Vera Cruz, some of *Utah*'s 17 officers and 367 sailors comprising a bluejacket "battalion" sent ashore distinguished themselves; 7 were awarded Medals of Honor: Lieutenant Guy W.S. Castle, battalion commander; company commanders Ensigns Oscar C. Badger II and Paul F. Foster; section leaders Chief Turret Captains Niels Drustrup and Abraham Desomer; Chief Gunner George Bradley; and Boatswain's Mate Henry N. Nickerson. The *Utah*, commissioned into the Atlantic Fleet on August 31, 1911, was frequently at Hampton Roads for port calls and exercises. It was later sunk during the Japanese attack on Pearl Harbor on December 7, 1941.

The Victoria Hotel, situated at 359–361 East Main Street and built in 1907 during the Jamestown Exposition, is pictured circa 1912 and includes a glimpse of the Majestic Theatre two doors down on the right. The beautifully constructed Tudor Gothic façade of the theatre harked to its construction in 1850 as Mechanics Hall, a fashionable venue for socials and musicals until 1907, when it was renamed the Majestic. The Majestic featured vaudeville and burlesque until 1936, when it was reopened as the Gaiety Theatre, a burlesque house. The Victoria and Gaiety succumbed to downtown redevelopment in the early 1960s.

Confederate Civil War survivors held a memorial service honoring dead comrades on Memorial Day, May 18, 1922. This small gathering of gray-haired men, faltering as the years passed but whose eyes still burned with the same fire that brought them glory on the field of battle, stood tall to have their picture taken in Commercial Place. *Courtesy of the Sargeant Memorial Room, Norfolk Public Library.*

Carnation Milk
POLA NEGRI
THE SPANISH Dancer
MILLINERY SUPPLIES.
GRANBY

The Pennsylvania Railroad maintained a ticket office on the ground floor of the old Neddo Hotel at the time this picture was taken about 1927. The Neddo Hotel, built in 1902, was located on East Plume Street. The hotel was razed in 1979.

Opposite, top: Thrift Millinery Supplies occupied the northwest corner of Granby and Freemason Streets from 1924 (when this picture was taken) to 1927; it was gone in 1928. The Granby Theatre, which made its debut in 1917, is down the street.

Opposite, bottom: News that Henry Ford had chosen Norfolk as the site for the largest automobile assembling and distribution plant on the Atlantic Coast was first announced on December 7, 1921, on the front page of Norfolk newspapers. The Ford Motor Company, Norfolk Assembly Plant, was constructed on a fifty-one-acre tract in Newton Park beginning in 1924. The first Norfolk-built Ford was a Model T produced in April 1925. City of Norfolk mayor Stockton Heth Tyler took delivery of the car at the plant in the presence of (from left) Dr. P.S. Schenck, director of Public Welfare and Health; J. Watts Martin, Norfolk City Council member; Howard G. Martin, executive vice-president of Merchants and Planters Bank; E. Jeff Robertson, Norfolk vice mayor; Charles B. Borland, director of Public Safety; Charles Herbert, Norfolk councilman; and W.W. Mitchell, plant manager. Mayor Tyler is at the wheel. The Norfolk Ford Plant closed in 2007.

Norfolk's Union Street Station opened on May 31, 1912, as a passenger terminal for three railroads: Norfolk and Western, the Virginian and Norfolk Southern. The station's first master was George C. Gill. Above the ground-level terminal were seven floors of railroad offices. This picture shows the station on October 28, 1933. Located at the foot of East Main Street and Lake (later Lovitt) Avenue, the station was convenient to car and foot traffic. Union Street Station was razed in March 1963. *Courtesy of the Norfolk and Western Collection, Virginia Polytechnic Institute and State University.*

Opposite, top: The elegantly appointed waiting room of the Union Street Station was photographed by Harry Mann just after the terminal opened in the spring of 1912.

The new City Market addition was photographed under construction on November 1, 1922. Benjamin F. Mitchell was the architect of record, and Baker & Brinkley built it. This addition was finished in 1923 at a cost of $500,000.

Mennonite farmers opened stalls outside the main City Market and Armory, but later a number of them moved inside the new City Market addition. They sold dairy products, eggs, preserves and vegetables. This picture was taken in 1937.

A great snowstorm struck the city on March 10, 1934, but its huge flakes disappeared as soon as they touched the ground. By nightfall there was little evidence of snow, except trace amounts on lawns and fields. But it was messy. Six to eight inches had fallen, melted away and frozen over on streets. Answering duty's call was this traffic officer at the intersection of Granby Street and City Hall Avenue. *Courtesy of the Sargeant Memorial Room, Norfolk Public Library.*

Opposite, bottom: Buchanan's Seafood Restaurant at 151 Granby Street, shown on this advertising card, opened in 1927 and closed in 1931. The restaurant was owned by John T. and Roland Buchanan and Clayton E. Rabey. The Buchanan brothers, including another brother, Ivison, had been in the seafood and wild game business in the City Market—John W. Buchanan and Sons, started by their father—from 1897 to 1927.

The Colonial Theatre was built as a legitimate theatre house in 1906. Located at 108–120 West Tazewell Street, directly behind the Lorraine Hotel, the Colonial made its debut during the Jamestown Exposition with a live stage production of *Pocahontas*. Later, the Colonial hosted such vaudeville legends as Al Jolson, Harry Houdini, Fred and Adele Astaire and Mae West. From the 1930s to the early 1970s, the Colonial was given an Art Deco face-lift and converted to a movie theatre. When this photograph was taken about 1935, iconic American child actress Shirley Temple was the star attraction. The Colonial Theatre was demolished in 1997.

The Hub men's clothing store was owned and operated by Charles and Louis Mansbach from 1907, when they acquired the shop from a Russian immigrant named Harry Wurtzburger and his son, David, who worked for his father from 1899 to 1906. The original Hub was on East Main Street near Church Street until 1927, when the Mansbachs moved the business to the Spratley Building on the northeast corner of Granby and Tazewell Streets. Charles Borjes took this picture of the Hub in 1927, just after the move took place. *Courtesy of the Sargeant Memorial Room, Norfolk Public Library.*

Charles Borjes took this picture of the Granby Theatre on February 28, 1937, during a showing of the *Cavalcade of Stars*, a touring stage show. Will Rogers's image is across the marquee. The Granby opened in 1917 as a moving picture house. Along with the Strand and Wells, it showed the first picture shows in Norfolk. *Courtesy of the Sargeant Memorial Room, Norfolk Public Library.*

CAVALCADE
OF STARS
CAVALCADE OF STARS
ANGUS / SEARLE TWINS
Granby
COOPER'S
FOWLERS
OPTICAL PARLOR

UNDER-GRAD
CORNER

The Algonquin
RESTAURANT

Charles S. Borjes took this photograph of the 300 block of Granby Street in January 1948. The Loew's Theatre opened in 1925 as a movie palace (left) and was playing *Secret at the Door* starring Joan Bennett and Michael Redgrave. The architect for the twenty-five-hundred-seat theatre was Thomas White Lamb of New York, a nationally known theatre designer. *Courtesy of the Sargeant Memorial Room, Norfolk Public Library.*

Opposite, top: The Hub featured an "Undergrad Corner" for college-bound young men (shown here), as well as finely tailored men's professional and casual clothing. Charles Borjes snapped this picture in 1930. *Courtesy of the Sargeant Memorial Room, Norfolk Public Library.*

Opposite, bottom: The Algonquin Hotel had moved into the 1923 City Market addition at Monticello Avenue and Tazewell Streets when this photograph was taken in 1944. The saying carved in the face of the building read: "That pure food may be kept in the best manner and sold at a fair price, this building is erected by the City of Norfolk."

SUBURBIA

After Norfolk's first electric streetcars were introduced in 1888, the years that followed were energized by their appearance, sparking a period of intense land speculation, best seen in the large number of newly planned residential suburban developments called "streetcar suburbs." This suburbanization driven by streetcars, also called trolleys, lasted through 1930. Streetcars were larger and faster, but more significantly, they drove development past old city centers, elongating the profile and appearance of traditional retail and commercial corridors along their routes. These suburbs ranged in size from five or ten blocks of residential development to completely planned suburban communities providing commercial, residential and educational amenities.

New Norfolk suburbs used broad boulevards, wide streets and small parks in their designs. The earliest of Norfolk's true suburbs was Brambleton, where homes were built for the moderately well-to-do and which came into existence in an earlier era of suburbanization called the "town and country" period. These suburbs were extended relatively short distances from city centers and were typically accessed by horse-drawn carriages and streetcars. These were elegant, tree-lined areas. An 1853 description of Church Street observed "a handsomely paved street from the lower termination near the courthouse to the Town Bridge, with fine residences on the north." There was a push by established Norfolk families to escape the city center starting in the mid-nineteenth century, especially where historically significant residential areas were periodically allowed to drift into senescence.

Brambleton began to develop in the early nineteenth century, when there were more homes than shops on Church Street and when East Main and Holt Streets were high on the list of desirable residential districts. Brambleton developed successfully ahead of Ghent by nearly a century. Atlantic City, which played such an important role in Norfolk's—and Ghent's—history, was an established hub in the cotton industry; thus, its residences, including single-family homes and tenements, churches and businesses, catered almost exclusively to cotton industry workers and their families.

Suburbanization, at any given time and place, depends wholly on transportation and the length and breadth of the suburban ring from the heart of the city. In 1815, there were nice homes on Norfolk's Main Street, and residents were satisfied that they lived in the best part of town. But by 1836, Freemason Street had become the fashionable address, and it was then that commercial storefronts gobbled up beautifully appointed Colonial- and Georgian-era homes on Main Street, most of which were razed to make way for commodious new buildings that would eventually succumb to grander structures in the late nineteenth and early twentieth centuries. Until 1869, it appeared that residences would continue to be scattered around downtown, as public transportation was not yet available and only businessmen who could afford a horse and carriage dared build a house farther than a mile from the city center. In that year, 1869, the Norfolk City Railroad Company laid down tracks over the length of Main Street—east to west—and streetcars drawn by horses or mules soon jogged not only there but also along Church and Granby Streets. When streetcars moved out to Park Avenue, Brambleton came into its own. This process of movement out from the city center via the streetcar is evident in the history of all of Norfolk's earliest residential sections, from Brambleton, Atlantic City and Ghent to Park Place, Lambert's Point, Virginia Place, Colonial Place, Riverview and Larchmont and following a northward course to Bay View, Willoughby and Ocean View, the city's diverse communities fronting the Chesapeake Bay.

Reservoir Avenue in Norfolk's Brambleton residential section is pictured on this early divided back postcard, circa 1910. Views of Norfolk's first suburb are rare. Brambleton began to develop in the early nineteenth century during an earlier era of suburbanization called the "town and country" period. Brambleton was a short distance from downtown and typically accessed by horse-drawn carriages and, later, streetcars.

The corner of Clay and Claiborne Avenues in Brambleton, circa 1910, was filled with beautiful homes and happy children. Brambleton during this time had magnificent rose gardens, wooded lots and chicken yards.

Saint Mark's Episcopal Church was located on Myers Avenue (later Hampton Boulevard). Harry Mann photographed Reverend Edward Patton Miner on the steps of the church in 1907, shortly after he came over from Saint Luke's as Saint

Mark's rector. Saint Mark's ceased operation at this location in 1931, and the building was no longer used as a church after 1944. The building stood into the 1980s, when it was razed.

The Hampton Roads Yacht Club, headquartered at Willoughby, burned to the ground on September 3, 1913. The building shown here (left) was built in 1904, replacing a simpler structure (right), which became a boathouse for the club.

Prize cups won by the Hampton Roads Yacht Club at Saint Michael's, Maryland, in 1908 are shown on this postcard. The Hampton Roads Yacht Club's burgee, handmade by George Curtis, is today used by the Norfolk Yacht and Country Club, which adopted the flag after members of his club joined the Norfolk country club in the years following the fire that took their clubhouse at Willoughby.

Norfolk Fire Department Chemical Company No. 7 was located on Old Ocean View Road circa 1912, when Harry Mann took this picture of firefighters with their REO Motor Company fire truck. REO trucks were mounted with a combination of acetylene headlights and kerosene lamps for sidelights placed on either side of the radiator grill.

J.J. Morse's Store and Post Office was photographed for this Chessler Company postcard, circa 1910. This is a particularly rare subject and view of an old Ocean View storefront. John J. Morse's grocery store was a popular gathering spot for Ocean View residents.

Opposite, top: By the time Ernest L. Long, of Long's Studio, took this picture of Fourth of July bathers and strollers in 1929, Ocean View had already become a major resort destination. With the construction of the first rail connection there in 1878, the Norfolk & Ocean View Railroad Company developed the area quickly, building a hotel and pavilions, a boardwalk and, eventually, the Ocean View Amusement Park. More hotels, boardinghouses, restaurants, bars and businesses followed.

Opposite, bottom: Napoleon Bonaparte Joynes's mansion was built between 1913 and 1914 at 104 La Valette Avenue in the city's Riverview community adjacent to Lafayette Park. The home had about forty rooms, which Joynes, a popular and politically powerful saloonkeeper in Norfolk's predominantly black Fourth Ward, needed. He had six sons: Benjamin Sales, Herbert Smith, Dallis Brooks, Napoleon Jr., Thomas Wilcox and Vincent. In later years, four generations of the Joynes family lived there at one time. Joynes, the son of Washington and Martha Joynes, was born and raised in Norfolk's Second Ward. Harry Mann took this photograph in 1915. The home is no longer standing.

BOATING & FISHING
O.V. 106
Long Photo
NORFOLK, VA.

Top: Virginia Electric and Power Company (VEPCO) Bus No. 148 was making its way down Colley Avenue when this picture was taken in August 1931. The Colley Avenue Poultry Market is in the background.

Bottom: Divers Grocery, located at 3820 Granby Street, featured "Everything Good to Eat," including a full-service delicatessen and seafood counter, sandwiches so good that they made your mouth water, soft drinks, ice cream and candy. Charles S. Borjes took this picture of Divers, circa 1933. *Courtesy of the Sargeant Memorial Room, Norfolk Public Library.*

Opposite, top: Holloman-Brown Funeral Home occupied a stately Victorian-style home at the corner of Granby and Twenty-ninth Streets in the Park Place neighborhood when Charles S. Borjes took this picture on October 7, 1936. *Courtesy of the Sargeant Memorial Room, Norfolk Public Library.*

Looking north on Granby Street at Lafayette Park, Charles S. Borjes took this picture of a brisk, busy street scene on December 27, 1930. *Courtesy of the Sargeant Memorial Room, Norfolk Public Library.*

When Orlando Loiercio came to Norfolk in 1942 from New York City, he opened two restaurants. The first, on West Main Street next to Selden Arcade, was the Italian Kitchen; the second was the Napoli on Colley Avenue. He asked an artist and Russian Jew named Irving H. Wolshin to paint murals depicting Venice, Italy, for the Main Street restaurant's walls. Wolshin, a set painter for Fox Studios in Hollywood, complied. Loiercio consolidated and moved to 4024 Granby Street, shown here, in 1946 and renamed the restaurant the Venice, later the Veneziano.

Opposite, top: The Granby Street Bridge over Tanner's Creek, looking north, had a center lane for the trolley. The road and bridge to the Lakewood section are to the right. This picture was taken on February 5, 1938, by a Norfolk Police Department photographer. *Courtesy of the Sargeant Memorial Room, Norfolk Public Library.*

Opposite, bottom: The 4000 block of Granby Street was choked with automobiles when Charles Borjes took this picture on September 24, 1946. *Courtesy of the Sargeant Memorial Room, Norfolk Public Library.*

Orlando Loiercio died on April 2, 1952, during renovations to the Venice; he was fifty-four years old. His widow, Caterina, took over operation of the restaurant with their daughter, Angelina, and Angelina's husband, Antonino. C.S. Barrett took this picture during the "reopening" night celebration, post-renovations, in 1953. Caterina Loiercio is at far right, behind the counter. She passed away on December 5, 1981. *Courtesy of Angelina and Antonino Loiercio.*

The Venice's waitresses were photographed by C.S. Barrett during the restaurant's "reopening" night in 1953. They were family, Angelina Loiercio said later. Many of them worked for her father and mother. Today, the Venice is the Veneziano. The restaurant continues to be owned and operated by the Loiercio family. *Courtesy of Angelina and Antonino Loiercio.*

The Riverview Theatre had been open only a short time when Charles S. Borjes took this photograph on October 17, 1947. On the marquee was the movie *Cry Wolf*, starring Errol Flynn and Barbara Stanwyck. *Courtesy of the Sargeant Memorial Room, Norfolk Public Library.*

Norfolk Southern Railway rail buses began operations in 1935 from Norfolk to Virginia Beach. These rail buses were photographed at Norfolk's Park Avenue in 1935. Rail buses continued service in Norfolk until 1948. *Courtesy of the Sargeant Memorial Room, Norfolk Public Library.*

Ledger-Dispatch photographer H.D. Vollmer took this picture looking east on York Street between Yarmouth and Duke Streets in 1939, and years later he left a record of an Englishman who came to Norfolk after trying his fortune in California's French Gulch gold mine. Edward Sard Acton came to Norfolk in 1914; he was an upholsterer. By the time this photograph was taken, he had opened E.S. Acton Antiques at 266 West York Street, which also provided upholstery, refinishing and repair services. *Courtesy of Carroll H. Walker.*

Top: The Norfolk Police Department blocked southbound traffic on Granby to facilitate vehicular flow away from Monticello Avenue, which had been closed at the Norfolk and Western rail bridge. Traffic headed south on Granby was sent to Omohundro Avenue. Jim Mays took this picture in 1950. Granby curves past Broadway Street (right foreground where the car is turning in front of the Central Radio Company) before it straightens out again at Lafayette Park. *Courtesy of the Sargeant Memorial Room, Norfolk Public Library.*

Bottom: Trinity Lutheran Church was first organized on May 30, 1920, and located at Thirty-fourth Street and Omohundro Avenue. In May 1940, a new site was acquired on Granby Street in West Belvedere, where construction of the church shown here was begun in September 1944. It was finished in 1945, about the time this picture was taken. Reverend Paul A. Plawin, pastor from 1931 to 1966, oversaw this and other construction during his tenure.

Opposite, bottom: H.D. Vollmer of the Norfolk *Ledger-Dispatch* took this picture looking west on York Street between Boush and Duke Streets in 1946. *Courtesy of Carroll H. Walker.*

Carolton Oaks School, antecedent of Norfolk Collegiate School, was first opened on March 1, 1948, by Kate Stallings Jennings and Margaret Grigg Moore. Between 1951 and 1952, Jennings and Moore developed the property at 7336 Granby Street, and on May 23, 1954, the building shown here was completed and opened. It has since succumbed to Norfolk Collegiate's state-of-the-art middle and upper school campus. The lone survivor from this 1955 photograph is the loblolly pine planted by Jennings and Moore. It stands in Norfolk Collegiate's upper school courtyard.

Saint Vincent DePaul Hospital left its old site on Church Street in early 1944 and moved to its present location at Granby Street and Kingsley Lane (shown here), when its name also changed to DePaul Hospital. The hospital is shown under construction in this Charles S. Borjes photograph, taken on May 5, 1944. *Courtesy of the Sargeant Memorial Room, Norfolk Public Library.*

The intersection of Granby Street and Little Creek Road that is today the heart of Norfolk's Ward's Corner section looked very different circa 1939, when this photograph was taken of A.C. Ward's earliest business venture at the corner that still bears his name. The Little Giant Market with Texaco gas pumps occupied 7601 Granby Street. *Courtesy of the Sargeant Memorial Room, Norfolk Public Library.*

Leap-the-Dips (shown here) rollercoaster was the star attraction at the Ocean View Amusement Park. Jim Mays took this picture on April 1, 1950. *Courtesy of the Sargeant Memorial Room, Norfolk Public Library.*

Opposite, bottom: Browney's, located at 1872 East Little Creek Road, was once one of north Norfolk's most popular restaurants, known for its seafood, prime western steaks and southern fried chicken. Browney's, shown here circa 1970, is gone, but the memories remain.

Mason's Eastern Shore Seafood Restaurant was located at 4019 Granby Street and is shown on this linen postcard mailed on February 29, 1952. This was not the first Mason's in Norfolk. Mason Brothers' Seafood Restaurants were opened at 215 Monticello Avenue from 1926 to 1929; 110 College Place in 1929; and after 1931, at 151 Granby Street. The "brothers" were Crisfield, Maryland natives George McClellan, James Henry and William Paul Mason. George's son, Linford, waited tables at his father's restaurants before owning his own, the Mason's shown here, which closed for good in 1979. Linford died on November 24, 2008, at age ninety-seven.

LOST NORFOLK

After its early twentieth-century zenith, sections of Norfolk began to fade quickly with the economic slump of the Great Depression and commensurate social downturn that followed World War II, periods that brought different challenges to city leaders. While slum clearance was discussed widely before the war, it could not be addressed fully until the fighting ended. Construction of housing for defense workers and military service members started before the Japanese attack on Pearl Harbor and continued to be Norfolk's top priority during the war years. It was not until 1951 that the City of Norfolk started the conversion of slum areas to public housing units for people who had previously lived in dilapidated sections of the downtown area. Low-cost, subsidized housing sprung up where slums once stood. But it was congressional redevelopment legislation that had the greatest impact on the face of downtown's central business district and waterfront.

Two decisions played a critical role: Congress removed the restriction that cleared slum areas could be used only for public housing, and, believing that the federal law would be amended thusly, Norfolk Housing Authority director Lawrence Cox requested that the 1946 Virginia General Assembly pass an enabling act to permit Virginia localities to benefit from the congressional bill. On November 14, 1945, legislation was introduced before the U.S. Senate to expand the country's public housing program and establish a five-year program for urban redevelopment. This legislation became known as the Wagner-Ellender-Taft Bill; it passed on March 13, 1946, and became

Virginia Redevelopment Law. Under the federal bill, housing authorities where states passed enabling legislation were empowered to acquire, clear and make available to private developers blighted areas for redevelopment. The Norfolk Housing Authority had already been able to make land available for public uses that were consistent with the city land-use plan, thus enabling it to proceed with the condemnation of vast acreage at the east end of downtown and beyond to construct a new civic center, public safety building and the like. After Virginia passed its enabling legislation, Norfolk Housing Authority became the Norfolk Redevelopment and Housing Authority (NRHA).

Though areas of downtown, Church Street and Huntersville fared well enough until post World War II, their ultimate decline can be traced to three major factors that occurred between 1947 and 1965: "white flight" from the city center and early city suburbs; the increased mobility and growing affluence of African Americans, influenced by opportunities brought about during the peak of the civil rights movement and African Americans' growing acceptance of living in outlying suburbia; and the severance of lower Church Street with the construction of the Downtown Plaza Shopping Center, a decision that effectively halved the street and cut it off from its southern terminus. Another factor often overlooked in the decline of the Church Street and Huntersville area at this time was the loss of community. As middle- and upper-income African Americans moved away from Church Street, lower-income individuals and families were left behind, most of them struggling without the benefit of financial stability created by the community reinvestment of middle- and upper-income blacks that buttressed capital improvements and safe conditions in which to live and work. Gone, too, were the community leaders and success stories that followed them in the public eye, people who could keep Church Street's best and brightest young people from slipping into obscurity—or worse, into the world of drugs, crime and mischief—by their powerful example of good fortune and social mores.

Redevelopment Project No. 1 got underway on December 11, 1951, the date that the first slum structure was demolished and one that is now recognized as the start of redevelopment in the United States. The first dwelling razed was at 755 Smith Street, just outside Norfolk's downtown central business district, more often referred to as the financial district, and now located within the Young Park public housing complex. Norfolk was the first city in the country to implement wholesale urban redevelopment. Many of the properties declared blighted were historically and architecturally significant structures condemned because they sat next to a dilapidated neighbor or sat in the path of private development. The city's first redevelopment project, which was not phased out until 1964, cleared 127 acres of downtown and cleared land for thirty new commercial buildings built by private developers; the Golden Triangle Motor Hotel was one of them. The project to follow, on the northwest boundary of downtown, occurred in Atlantic City and involved the extension of Hampton Boulevard to the Midtown Tunnel; created a medical center complex around Norfolk General Hospital; provided land for Eastern Virginia Medical School; and made property available to private developers for apartment buildings and commercial storefronts. Demolition started in Atlantic City on September 26, 1957, and cleared 140 acres, razing 361 structures. With the exception of two homes, all the dwellings within the Atlantic City boundary were built prior to World War I.

Further, there was a laundry list of projects that, in their planning, were not intended to end the important contribution of East Main and Church Streets and Commercial Place but did. The completion of the Norfolk–Portsmouth Bridge-Tunnel and new Berkley Bridge enabled downtown commuters to bypass Norfolk's east-end commercial corridor. Urban renewal projects in the 1950s and early 1960s cleared over two hundred acres of downtown Norfolk, thus eliminating the connection between the city center and Church Street. In July 1956, a master plan for Norfolk's central business district was announced that initiated Downtown Redevelopment Project North and South, which contained 838 residential and commercial structures. NRHA started demolition on July 30, 1958, beginning with the old National Hotel that stood on an East Main Street lot that was set aside for a new public safety building. On June 27, 1961, the Norfolk City Council added Downtown Redevelopment Project East. Bulldozers moved in to clear twenty-one acres for the Downtown Plaza Shopping Center. Old streets were rerouted; others were cut off or eliminated to facilitate traffic between downtown and new facilities, including the medical center complex and Eastern Virginia Medical School. Thus, Saint Paul's Boulevard was laid down, Brambleton Avenue extended to Hampton Boulevard and Waterfront, later Waterside, Drive was constructed.

Despite Norfolk's expansive redevelopment program, the city center continued to struggle until the late twentieth century, when an infusion of investor capital led to permanent changes, including new residential and commercial buildings that brought an influx of downtown residents and new businesses. All of this, of course, followed on the heels of grass-roots initiatives like Harborfest, which brought Hampton Roads citizens back to Norfolk with a lively waterfront festival started in 1976, and the establishment of Town Point Park soon after. Evident today is the attempt to recreate what was, to design and build condominiums, apartment buildings, single-family homes and a festival marketplace reminiscent of the city's old ferry terminal building, all bearing architectural features that take us back to the glory days of old Norfolk and streetscapes that revive the appearance of the same. Norfolk revived passenger rail with a new light rail system in the twenty-first century, but it had passenger rail a half century ago—and a magnificent station at Union Street—before the building was razed and track pulled up during the rush to make everything old new again at the peak of postwar redevelopment. Today's downtown Norfolk is a wall of steel, glass and concrete office towers that give the appearance that the city did not exist until modern times. There are few remaining buildings that tether Norfolk to its roots as one of the East Coast's oldest and most important seaport cities.

Opposite, top: Charles Borjes took this picture of the first block of Granby Street looking north from the foot of West Main Street, circa 1946. *Courtesy of the Sargeant Memorial Room, Norfolk Public Library.*

Opposite, bottom: The *Norfolk Ledger-Dispatch* published this photograph of Brewer Street looking north from Brambleton Avenue on February 16, 1946. Much of this area was subsequently razed for redevelopment. *Courtesy of the Sargeant Memorial Room, Norfolk Public Library.*

SWATTY'S
PANTS
CHOP SUEY
VICTORY
RESTAURANT
GARDEN
RESTAURANT
ROXY
SALASKY
London Row
CLOTHES
ANNEX
HATS
TAVERN

NORFOLKS
LEADING
THEATRE
HOME OF
Metro Goldwyn Mayer
WOOLWORTH
F. W. WOOLWORTH CO.

A Rosedale Dairy driver stopped at a city trough for his horse to drink on a hot summer's day. Charles Borjes snapped this picture on August 5, 1949. Rosedale Dairy was located at 929–931 Monticello Avenue. Despite the growing popularity of milk delivery trucks, Rosedale continued to use horse-drawn delivery. *Courtesy of the Sargeant Memorial Room, Norfolk Public Library.*

Opposite, top: Colonel Charles Herbert Consolvo, owner of the Monticello Hotel since 1905, stood in his office on September 23, 1946, admiring the many photographs of people, places and events that decorated its walls. *Virginian-Pilot* photographer Charles S. Borjes took this picture, one of the last to be taken, of an ailing Consolvo. He died on October 24, 1947. *Courtesy of the Sargeant Memorial Room, Norfolk Public Library.*

Opposite, bottom: A fixture at the corner of Granby and Freemason Streets for decades, the F.W. Woolworth Company store was one of the last to close as Granby Street reached the peak of its decline. Charles Borjes took this photograph on December 18, 1948, capturing the hordes of Christmas shoppers that choked downtown during the holiday season. *Courtesy of the Sargeant Memorial Room, Norfolk Public Library.*

Rail workers pulled up streetcar tracks at City Hall Avenue and Bank Street in 1949.

This aerial view of Norfolk's future civic center site shows the area as it appeared prior to construction. The photo was taken in 1959. Norfolk Redevelopment and Housing Authority (NRHA) began demolition here on July 30, 1958. The first target was the old National Hotel, on an East Main Street site that would later become the civic center. The plan's objectives also called for a new city hall, a new public safety building, parking facilities, office buildings and a shopping center.

The 1961 completion of the public safety building marked the beginning of a $15 million civic center project that included a courts building and the eleven-story Norfolk City Hall by 1965. The year 1961 also marked the beginning of demolition of Norfolk's East Main Street saloons and strip clubs. This second aerial picture shows the public safety building immediately after completion.

Joynes Tire Company at Granby and Tenth Streets was started by Benjamin S. and Dallis B. Joynes, sons of Napoleon B. Joynes. Benjamin and Dallis brought brothers Napoleon Jr. and Vincent into the business as salesmen. The elder Joynes brothers did not enjoy long lives. Benjamin died in 1937 and Dallis in 1934. Joynes Tire Company was still in business in July 1959, when this picture was taken, despite the passing of Napoleon Jr. in 1950 and Vincent in 1953. *Courtesy of the Sargeant Memorial Room, Norfolk Public Library.*

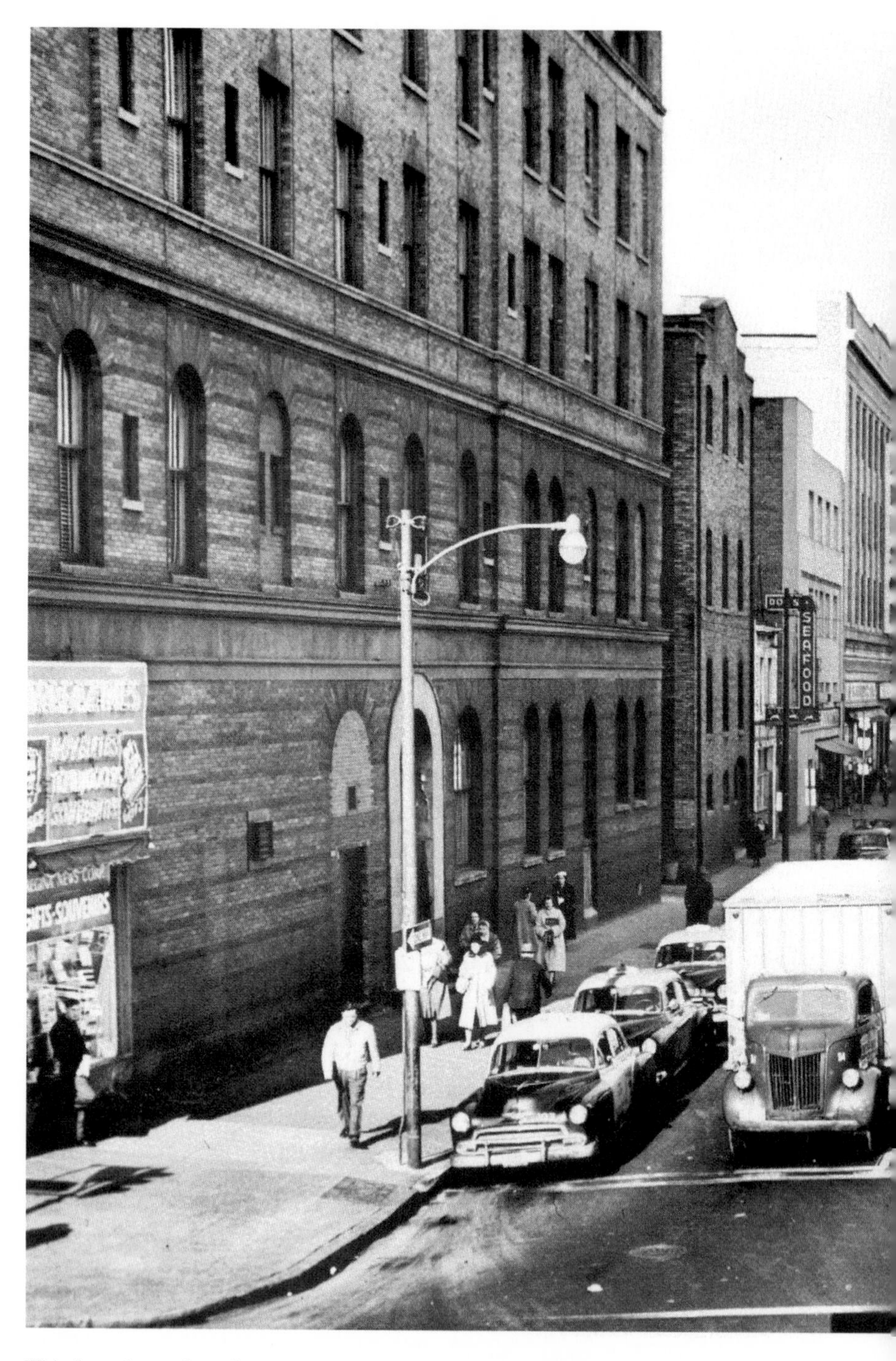

This first of two views demonstrates the dramatic change to Norfolk's downtown landscape post–World War II. Seldom seen is this rare view of an empty lot, circa 1958, where the City Market and Armory once stood and the Maritime Tower was

yet to be built. Looking north down Monticello Avenue, the Monticello Hotel is at left foreground, but note the Kresge store and W.T. Grant's beyond the hotel.

The second view of the former City Market and Armory site shows the Maritime Tower after completion, about 1960.

Opposite, top: Norfolk has held on to Doumar's, the curb service restaurant on Monticello Avenue and Twentieth Street, since 1934, when Abe Doumar consolidated two stands—one at Ocean View Amusement Park and the other on Virginia Beach's original boardwalk—to this location. Abe introduced the world to the ice cream cone at the Saint Louis Exposition in 1904. Abe came to Norfolk with his brother, George, during the Jamestown Exposition three years later and never left. Today's existing restaurant building was built in 1949. This picture, taken in 1957, shows George Doumar, Abe's brother, handing off an ice cream cone to waitress Inez Cuthrel as his sons, Al, John and Victor, look on. Abe's original four-iron cone-making machine is still used to make handmade ice cream cones.

Carroll H. Walker took this picture of Granby Street looking north from Brambleton Avenue on May 16, 1959. The Greyhound bus terminal is on the right.

Before and after photographs of the Kirn Memorial Library site are remarkably telling. The first photograph shows mid-nineteenth-century buildings in Norfolk's downtown redevelopment area on the site of what was planned as the city's new municipal library. The building nearest the foreground was once the A.C. Cox Grocery Company and was situated on the corner of Bank Street and East City Hall Avenue in 1930. A.C. Cox ceased operations in 1955.

By June 1959, Granby Street looking south from City Hall Avenue was no longer beckoning pedestrians. The Haddington Building, occupied by National Airlines, is at left. The F.S. Royster Building is at right (foreground). Down the end of the block, near the corner of Granby and West Main Streets, the third Atlantic Hotel loomed large. *Courtesy of the Sargeant Memorial Room, Norfolk Public Library.*

Opposite, bottom: Kirn Memorial Library, shown after it opened in 1962, served as the city's main branch for forty-seven years, until it was demolished over the summer of 2009 to make way for a light-rail station. Named for German immigrants Henry and Elizabeth Kirn, the library occupied a large footprint, facing East City Hall Avenue but bordered all around by Plume, Atlantic and Bank Streets. Norfolk's main library moved the historic Seaboard Building on Plume Street.

Kline Chevrolet used car dealership occupied an expansive and prominent lot between Granby Street (foreground) and Monticello Avenue, circa 1959. In the background at left is the Kramer Tire Company on Monticello Avenue, which is still in this location today.

James Murdaugh took this picture of the Greyhound bus station at the corner of Granby Street and Brambleton Avenue in February 1960. *Courtesy of the Sargeant Memorial Room, Norfolk Public Library.*

A January 1961 fire gutted the sixth floor of the Haddington Building at the corner of Granby Street and City Hall Avenue. Damage to the building was so extensive that it had to be closed. Carroll H. Walker took this picture of the Haddington on February 2, 1961. He called the picture "the end of the Haddington." *Courtesy of Carroll H. Walker.*

HOME OF
REYNOLD'S
HARDWARE CO.
Reynold's
HARDWARE CO.

Two views of Brambleton Avenue (the second is on the following page) show the transformation of one of Norfolk's most important transportation corridors. The first view, shown here, is Brambleton Avenue, formerly Queen Street, and Boush Street looking west before expansion and extension of the street to Hampton Boulevard. The street in the center is Dartmouth Street, which was later eliminated. Eugene G. Vickhouse took this photograph on January 27, 1960.

Opposite, top: When it opened in 1961 the Golden Triangle Motor Hotel was unlike any other hotel in town. New, modern and well appointed, it sat on five and a half acres of redeveloped land at Monticello and Brambleton Avenues. This picture was taken just after the hotel's opening. Visible at the bottom of the picture is Young Park public housing, started in 1951 during the first phase of Norfolk's slum conversion program. Young Park's first families moved in two years later.

Opposite, bottom: Carroll Walker took this picture of Market and Brewer Streets in 1960. *Courtesy of the Sargeant Memorial Room, Norfolk Public Library.*

This second view of Brambleton Avenue is looking toward The Hague on the right. George Haycox of Haycox Photographic took this picture on February 28, 1964.

Opposite, top: The 100 block of Granby Street looking north from Main Street toward Plume in April 1961 was dotted with delicatessens, taverns and businesses, none of which projected the elegance and propriety of turn-of-the-century shops and cafés. James Murdaugh's picture records the end of establishments like Sol's Delicatessen and Piedmont Airlines on Granby Street. *Courtesy of the Sargeant Memorial Room, Norfolk Public Library.*

Opposite, bottom: The Monticello Hotel was imploded on January 26, 1976, a moment preserved in this picture by Alexander P. Grice III. The U.S. Federal Building was built in its place. *Courtesy of Carroll H. Walker.*

PIEDMONT
AIRLINES
SOL'S
DELICATESSEN
RESTAURANT

CALL
MA 5 4406
MAURY'S

Architect Charles Ansell took this picture of the main elevation of the 1850 Norfolk City Hall and Courthouse, now the General Douglas MacArthur Memorial, in August 1981 as part of a Historic American Buildings Survey, America's City Halls Project. Located at 421 East City Hall Avenue, this structure was originally designed by William R. Singleton, a Portsmouth, Virginia native and Saint Louis architect, with assistance from Thomas U. Walter. It has been described as one of Virginia's best remaining Classical Revival buildings. *Courtesy of the Library of Congress Prints and Photographs Division.*

SELECTED BIBLIOGRAPHY

Primary Sources

Norfolk Redevelopment and Housing Authority (NRHA). "Facts about Granby Street." October 22, 1973.

Sanborn Fire Insurance Maps for Norfolk, Virginia.

Books

Art Works of Norfolk, Virginia, and Vicinity. Chicago, IL: W. Kennicott and Company, Publishers, 1895, 1902.

Chambers, Lenoir, and Joseph E. Shank. *Salt Water & Printer's Ink*. Chapel Hill, NC: University of North Carolina Press, 1967.

Forrest, William S. *Historical and Descriptive Sketches of Norfolk and Vicinity*. Philadelphia, PA: Lindsay and Blakiston, 1853.

Greeley, Horace, et al. *The Great Industries of the United States*. Hartford, CT: J.B. Burr and Hyde, 1873.

Hale, Jonathan. *The Old Way of Seeing*. Boston, MA: Houghton Mifflin Company, 1994.

Lamb, Robert W., ed. *Our Twin Cities of the Nineteenth Century: Norfolk and Portsmouth—Their Past, Present and Future*. Norfolk, VA: Barcroft, Publisher, 1887/8.

Loth, Calder, ed. *The Virginia Landmarks Register*. Charlottesville, VA: University Press of Virginia, 1987.

Martin-Perdue, Nancy J., and Charles L. Perdue Jr., eds. *Talk About Trouble: A New Deal Portrait of Virginians in the Great Depression*. Chapel Hill, NC: University of North Carolina Press, 1996.

Tazewell, William L. *Norfolk's Waters: An Illustrated Maritime History of Hampton Roads*. Woodland Hills, CA: Windsor Publications, 1982.

Tucker, George Holbert. *Norfolk Highlights 1584–1881*. Portsmouth, VA: Printcraft Press, 1972.

Walker, Carroll H. *Carroll Walker's Norfolk: A Tricentennial History*. Virginia Beach, VA: Donning, 1981.

———. *Norfolk: A Pictorial History*. Virginia Beach, VA: Donning, 1975.

Wertenbaker, Thomas J. *Norfolk: Historic Southern Port*. Durham, NC: Duke University Press, 1931.

Whichard, Rogers Dey. *The History of Lower Tidewater Virginia*, Vols. I–III. New York, NY: Lewis Historical Publishing Company, 1959.

Yarsinske, Amy Waters. *The Elizabeth River*. Charleston, SC: The History Press, 2007.

———. *Ghent: John Graham's Dream, Norfolk, Virginia's Treasure*. Charleston, SC: The History Press, 2006.

———. *The Jamestown Exposition: American Imperialism on Parade*, Vols. I and II. Charleston, SC: Arcadia, 1999.

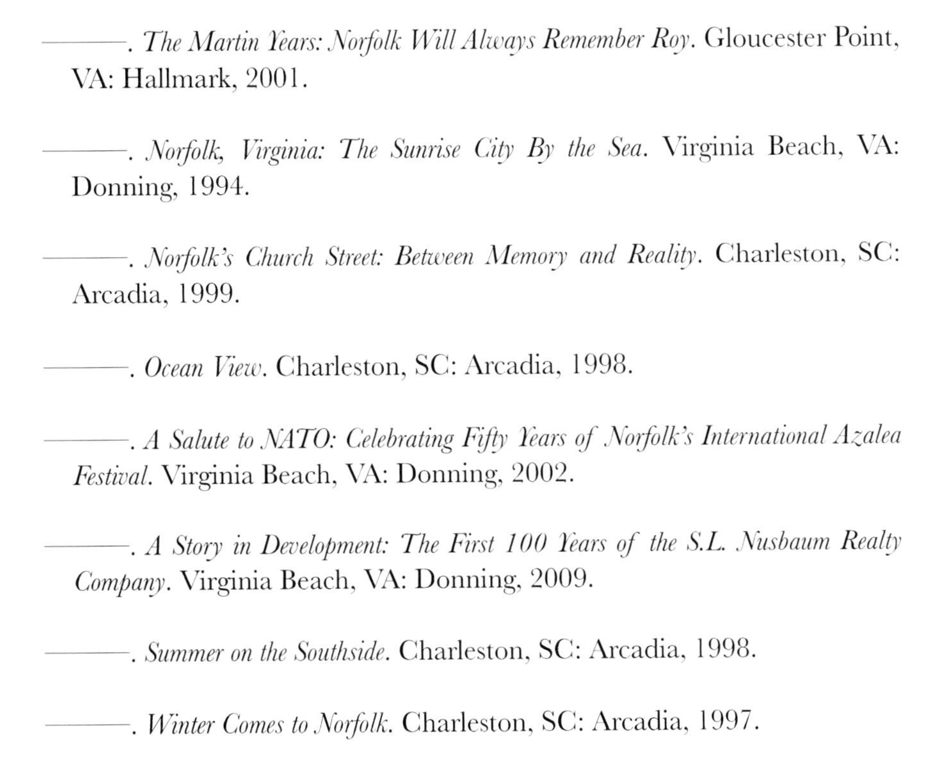

———. *The Martin Years: Norfolk Will Always Remember Roy*. Gloucester Point, VA: Hallmark, 2001.

———. *Norfolk, Virginia: The Sunrise City By the Sea*. Virginia Beach, VA: Donning, 1994.

———. *Norfolk's Church Street: Between Memory and Reality*. Charleston, SC: Arcadia, 1999.

———. *Ocean View*. Charleston, SC: Arcadia, 1998.

———. *A Salute to NATO: Celebrating Fifty Years of Norfolk's International Azalea Festival*. Virginia Beach, VA: Donning, 2002.

———. *A Story in Development: The First 100 Years of the S.L. Nusbaum Realty Company*. Virginia Beach, VA: Donning, 2009.

———. *Summer on the Southside*. Charleston, SC: Arcadia, 1998.

———. *Winter Comes to Norfolk*. Charleston, SC: Arcadia, 1997.

ARTICLES, ORAL HISTORIES, PAMPHLETS, PAPERS, REPORTS AND SPEECHES

There were numerous articles, brochures, pamphlets, meeting minutes and organization papers and broadsides that informed the author; some were dated, others were not. As many as possible are listed below, while others are sporadically included as textual reference.

Bancroft, Raymond L. "Granby could be Disneyland." *Virginian-Pilot*, April 17, 1964.

Bayer, Richard C. "Granby in holding action against urban decay peril." *Ledger-Star*, May 4, 1973.

Butler, Kathleen. "Working to stand out from the crowd." *Virginian-Pilot* and *Ledger-Star*, November 22, 1993.

Caflin, Arlette. "Pharmacy owner tries to keep aura intact." *Norfolk Compass*, July 5–6, 1989.

Carpenter, Brown. "Granby Mall: a beginning." *Ledger-Dispatch*, October 19, 1974.

Carpenter, Brown, and Harry Eagar. "Granby has labor pains awaiting birth." *Ledger-Dispatch*, May 10, 1975.

Cohn, Meredith. "Fix it and they will come." *Virginian-Pilot*, October 26, 1998.

Dinsmore, Christopher, and Meredith Kruse. "Granby location picked for site of Norfolk hotel." *Virginian-Pilot*, May 4, 2001.

Doucette, John-Henry. "Watching and waiting." *Virginian-Pilot*, October 27, 1998.

Fiske, Warren. "Great hopes not stirred." *Virginian-Pilot*, October 21, 1979.

Friddell, Guy. "Un-malling street." *Virginian-Pilot*, June 10, 1987.

Glass, Jon. "City revival agency will shore up its Granby Street home." *Virginian-Pilot*, June 17, 1997.

Goldblatt, Jennifer. "Betting on a grander Granby." *Virginian-Pilot*, October 25, 1998.

Kelley, George M. "Granby Street widening studied." *Virginian-Pilot*, January 12, 1955.

———. "Multi-million dollar project on Granby Street revealed." *Virginian-Pilot*, January 16, 1955.

Kennedy, Davis. "Face-lifting may start in 1967." *Virginian-Pilot*, December 1, 1966.

Knepler, Mike. "Downtown area wins historic tag." *Virginian-Pilot*, April 14, 1987.

———. "Granby upgrading viewed as a 2-way street." *Virginian-Pilot*, January 11, 1988.

———. "NRHA plan may uproot Granby Mall stores." *Norfolk Compass*, February 24, 1985.Langston, Janet,

Lassiter, Glenda, "Evaluator gives downtown Norfolk low rating." *Virginian-Pilot*, July 18, 1986.

Ledger-Dispatch. "Chamber directors favor lower Granby expansion." January 12, 1955.

———. "Famous old Norfolk places." November 11, 1938.

———. "Granby Street widening up again." January 12, 1955.

———. "Granby's 300 block on building spree." November 14, 1960.

Ledger-Star. "Boost for the Granby Street Plan." July 22, 1968.

Levin, John. "Real estate firms are groping to fit pieces of puzzle." *Virginian-Pilot*, September 1, 1984.

Lewis, Lloyd H. "1816 Granby Street report finds way to clerk's desk." *Ledger-Star*, November 16, 1962.

Marshall, Alex. "A Granby Street revival." *Virginian-Pilot* and *Ledger-Star*, August 21, 1995.

Melton, Bill. "Norfolk's redevelopment story is one of success." *Daily Press*, September 7, 1980.

Messina, Debbie. "Petition aims to save history." *Virginian-Pilot*, August 2, 2007.

Michaels, Harriette Nadel. "Memories of Granby Street and a summertime gone by." *Virginian-Pilot*, July 1, 2001.

Minium, Harry. "Residential complex planned for Granby." *Virginian-Pilot*, December 9, 2003.

New York Times. "Open new Naval Y.M.C.A." March 18, 1909.

Norfolk Compass. "Battle lines drawn over median strip." September 27–28, 1978.

Phillips, Joseph V. "Facelift changes outlook for mall." *Virginian-Pilot*, June 1, 1975.

Poyner, Charlene. "2-way traffic brightens the outlook for Granby Street." *Virginian-Pilot* and *Ledger-Star*, September 5, 1987.

Smith, Mike. "Stores closing despite mall." *Virginian-Pilot*, November 17, 1975.

South, Jeff. "For a 'dying' mall, Granby is 'terrific.'" *Ledger-Star*, August 8, 1981.

Stanus, Joan. "Closing the store." *Norfolk Compass*, April 28–29, 1993.

Sullivan, Frank. "Downtown Norfolk can 'support' imposing skyline, builder says." *Virginian-Pilot*, August 13, 1958.

Sumner, Grace. "'Brotherhood Boulevard' would be fitting name for northern Granby Street." *Ledger-Dispatch*, February 19, 1955.

Thompson, Rebecca. "A street at the crossroads: Granby after Woolworth's." *Virginian-Pilot* and *Ledger-Star*, March 27, 1989.

Tucker, George Holbert. "City grew around Granby Street." *Virginian-Pilot*, February 19, 1962.

———. "Granby Street salad days are now a memory." *Virginian-Pilot*, January 19, 1986.

———. "Lower Granby Street blends past, present." *Virginian-Pilot*, September 28, 1964.

Virginian-Pilot. "Big shade trees may come down." December 10, 1906.

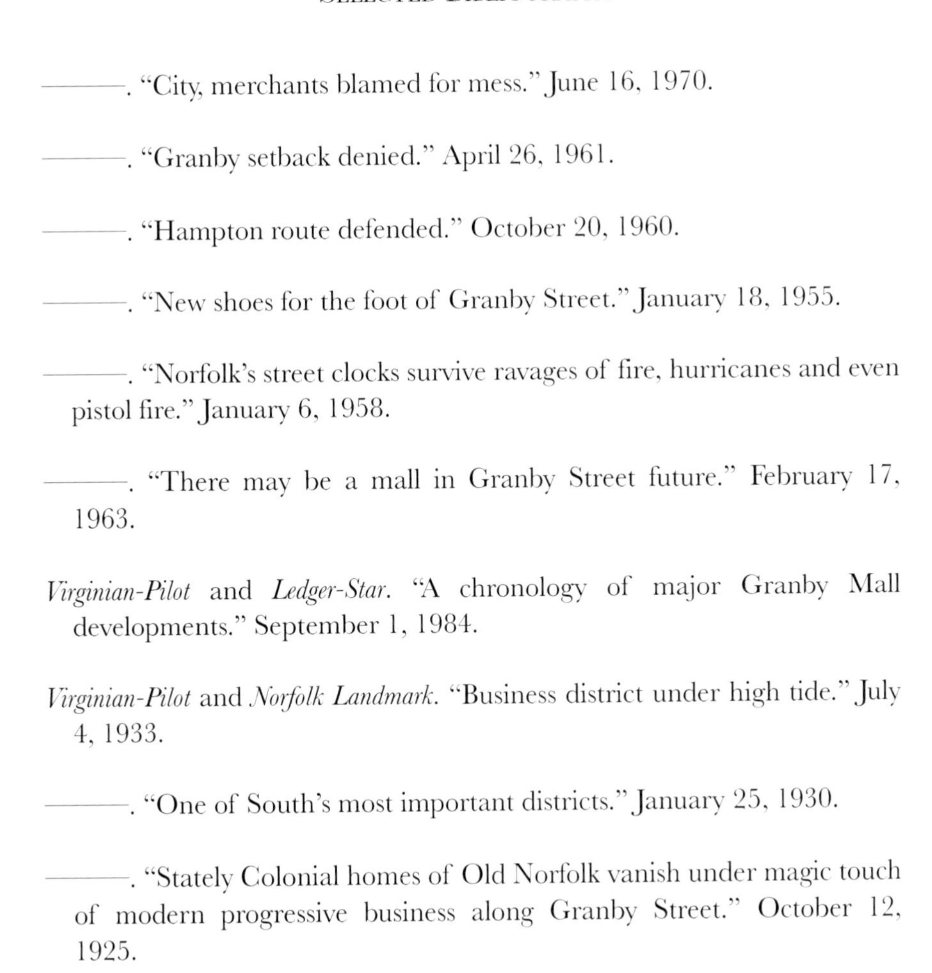

———. "City, merchants blamed for mess." June 16, 1970.

———. "Granby setback denied." April 26, 1961.

———. "Hampton route defended." October 20, 1960.

———. "New shoes for the foot of Granby Street." January 18, 1955.

———. "Norfolk's street clocks survive ravages of fire, hurricanes and even pistol fire." January 6, 1958.

———. "There may be a mall in Granby Street future." February 17, 1963.

Virginian-Pilot and *Ledger-Star*. "A chronology of major Granby Mall developments." September 1, 1984.

Virginian-Pilot and *Norfolk Landmark*. "Business district under high tide." July 4, 1933.

———. "One of South's most important districts." January 25, 1930.

———. "Stately Colonial homes of Old Norfolk vanish under magic touch of modern progressive business along Granby Street." October 12, 1925.

Witt, John. "Mall wilts as Norfolk blooms." *Richmond Times-Dispatch*, September 8, 1985.

Young, Sharon, and Warren Fiske. "Stirrings seen on Granby Mall." *Norfolk Compass*, October 22, 1983.

ABOUT THE AUTHOR

A nationally known, award-winning author of narrative nonfiction, Amy Waters Yarsinske received her master of planning degree from the University of Virginia School of Architecture and her bachelors of arts degrees in English and economics from Randolph-Macon Woman's College. She is a former president of the Norfolk Historical Society, cofounder of the Norfolk Historical Foundation and a graduate of CIVIC Leadership Institute. Yarsinske has over two decades of experience in the publishing industry as an author and editor and has made repeated appearances as a guest and commentator for major media, including American and foreign networks and international, national and regional radio markets. She is a member of Investigative Reporters and Editors (IRE), Authors Guild and American Society of Journalists and Authors (ASJA).

Yarsinske is the author of the widely read, award-winning *No One Left Behind: The Lt. Comdr. Michael Scott Speicher Story* (Dutton/NAL 2002, 2003; Listen and Live Audio, 2002, 2004, 2006; Topics Entertainment, 2004; Listen and Live Audio MP3, 2007). She has published two prior works with The History Press, *Ghent: John Graham's Dream, Norfolk, Virginia's Treasure* (2006) and *The Elizabeth River* (2007).